Jacob Berry Is "A Miracle On A Mission"
Spreading The Gospel Of Jesus Christ

LIVING
the GIFT

BRAND ARTIST
P R E S S

Living the Gift
The Autobiography of Jacob Berry

Published by Brand Artist Press,
with The Publishing Hub (www.thepublishinghub.com)

Unless otherwise noted, all Scripture quotations in this publication are from King James Version.

Printed in the United States of America

ISBN: 978-1-936417-59-9

Contact the author:

Jacob Berry
www.JacobBerryMinistries.org

Dedication

Dedicated in loving memory to:
Patsy Alliene (Ford) Berry August 9, 1924 - June 16, 2010

I wanted to dedicate this book, first and foremost, to my Lord and Savior, Jesus Christ, for with Him all things are made possible and also to my Grandma Berry, Patsy Alliene (Ford) Berry as she went home to be with our Heavenly Father during the writing of this book and, even though she wasn't here to witness the completion of this project, her prayers saw me through. If I had the opportunity to tell Grandma one more thing, it would be, "Thank you for praying for me and I will see you in the morning."

What Others are Saying

"Jacob Berry is living proof that God can use anyone who will willingly give himself fully to the Lord. His unique delivery and insight causes the Scriptures, even the most familiar ones, to come alive. God has given us the gift of physical life and spiritual life. Jacob is truly an example of one who is committed to Living The Gift." — *Rev. Sherman Branch*

The First Free Will Baptist Church Youth Group in Seffner, Florida wrote the following:

"I'm glad to say Jacob's my friend and a role model. God help me to have the drive and determination to serve the Lord like he does."

"Jacob has impacted my life like no other preacher, if he can serve God, I have no excuse, he's amazing and inspiring!"

"Jacob is a pint sized powerhouse for the Lord."

"Jacob is the opposite of handicapped—he can do things and reach those that others can't."

"Don't let his looks fool you, he's a normal guy, with an extraordinary gift from God. I'm amazed at how Jacob speaks right to the hearts of young people. There's no doubt God's hand and anointing are upon this young man and his ministry. He has impacted our youth group in a special way. Once you meet him, you'll gain a friend and never be the same!"

Contents

Preface

What an honor it is to write a few words about this great outreach ministry of literature by one of America's premier preachers, Jacob Berry. He may not be able to physically walk but I assure you he will leave giant footprints in your heart from his writings and ministry. God has gifted him as an evangelist for these days. His words are not idle and every thought is soaked in prayer. The anointing of the Holy Spirit on his life will be self evident as you read this book. It will be an investment of time you won't regret. So, read and be blessed by a life touched by God!

Dr. Calvin Ray Evans
Rubyville Community Church, Pastor
Evangelistic Outreach Ministries, Director

Foreword

Through the years, there have been many opinions on the Apostle Paul's "thorn in the flesh," but most Bible scholars believe that it was a severe physical infirmity. We can see that Paul prayed for healing, and we know that God spoke with him about it. The following words demonstrate his resulting confidence: *"For this thing I besought the Lord thrice, that it might depart from me. And he said unto me, my grace is sufficient for thee: for my strength is made perfect in weakness. Most gladly therefore will I rather glory in my infirmities, that the power of Christ may rest upon me."* — (2 Corinthians 12:8-9)

To a great extent, this is also Evangelist Jacob Berry's story. Although he has suffered with Muscular Dystrophy from birth, his life has been an example of God's powerful, triumphant grace. And even though Jacob was not even expected to live at first, spiritually he has soared like the eagles of Isaiah 40:31. From a young age, he embraced God's call to preach and as a result has proclaimed the Gospel to thousands, leaving no doubt in anyone's mind that the power of Christ is resting upon him.

Samuel B. McGinn
Senior Ministry Correspondent & Staff Pastor
Samaritan's Purse
Boone, North Carolina

Introduction

At first glance of me, people see a wheelchair, ventilator and a disability, but that is not what God sees.

> "... for the LORD seeth not as man seeth; for man looketh on the outward appearance, but the LORD looketh on the heart."
> — 1 Samuel 16:7 (KJV)

God sees past all my disabilities and He sees my heart.

I pray that, as you read my life's story, you also will see past my disabilities and see my heart.

During my life's story you may find happiness, sadness, excitement, and sometimes even humor, but whatever you may find, I pray that in the end, you will find the precious gift that God has given me which is salvation, life abundantly and everlasting through His son, Jesus Christ.

1

My Godly Heritage

I was blessed to have roots in a God-fearing, Christ-honoring heritage.

My paternal great grandfather was a praying man. He loved to go to church and loved Jesus with all of his heart. Of his many sons, he had one named Dean Berry who married a young, feisty woman, Patsy Ford who had a strong lineage of Cherokee Indian. My Grandpa and Grandma Berry had seven children. The youngest of these seven was named Joe Keith Berry, my dad. The Berry family resided in Grove, Oklahoma.

Thirty miles away, in Miami, Oklahoma, Fred George Mercer, a poor lead and zinc miner, married Hattie Bell

Hollis. They had nine children, one being, my maternal grandpa, Jackie Eldon Mercer, or as he is known, Jack. Jack would meet and marry a young woman in his hometown by the name of Donna Jean Hallman. They would go on to have two children, a boy and a girl. The girl was named Yvonne Lynn Mercer, my mom.

My dad was raised to be a hard worker and began work as an electrician and environmental control technician directly out of high school. My mom was a math whiz and used those skills to work at a local bank.

My mom and dad met in the summer of 1987. During this time in their life, my parents had drifted from their Godly heritage. I believe that it could only be through the prayers of my paternal grandmother and maternal grandpa and nanny that two unlikely people with Godly backgrounds could meet in a worldly situation.

My mom and dad got married on November 7, 1987, at an outdoor country style wedding at the home of my mom's brother and his wife, Randy and Donna Mercer.

My parents made their home in my mom's hometown, the rural community of Miami, Oklahoma. They continued living their life outside the will of God, but eleven months later that was all about to change.

2

An Unordinary Birth of an Extraordinary Life

J anuary 1988, Ronald Reagan is in the White House. The Washington Redskins were the defending Super Bowl champions; the most electrifying runner in college football, Barry Sanders of Oklahoma State, won the Heisman trophy; and the Showtime Lakers were the biggest thing in basketball. Americans were experimenting with new technology getting ready to step into a new decade. In the small town of Miami, Oklahoma, Joe and Yvonne Berry, my dad and mom, were getting ready to step into parenthood as they received confirmation that my mom was expecting a child, me.

My mother and father had always dreamed of having a child and taking that child to Sunday School and Church, even though at this point in their lives, they were still outside the will of God. They never realized that their dream would turn into something extraordinary and impact not only their future, but the future of many other lives.

The first few weeks into the pregnancy, there was a scare of a miscarriage, but God, as he would continue to do so many times, spared my life. The next few months of my mom's pregnancy seemed normal. However, as the months wore on, I continued to grow, but not progress. During the months that I should have started moving within the womb, my mom felt no movement, no kicking, no elbows; she only felt my hiccups after she had eaten pizza. My mom knew that there was something seriously wrong, but as Mary, she kept these things and pondered them in her heart, revealing them to no man, not even her husband.

It was during this troublesome time that my dad took my mom to the Berry family reunion. It was the first time for my mom to meet many of my dad's relatives, including my Great Grandpa Berry, who at this time was in the last stages of Alzheimer's disease. He may not have known his own children or who anybody else was who was talking to him that day during the reunion, but he knew exactly who was speaking to him through the inspiration of the Holy Ghost as he felt the urge to stretch forth his hand and to lay hands on me in my mother's womb and pray. My Great Grandpa knew exactly who was talking to him and who he was talking to that day. It is said even to this day in my family, "You should have heard Grandpa pray, for he was a man that could pray Heaven down. He was a man that, when he prayed, all of Heaven listened." Years later, as mom and dad shared this precious moment with me, Daddy said, "Grandpa might not have known what had happened yesterday, but he knew who held tomorrow."

My due date of October 12, 1988 came and went. So on October 17, 1988, my mom was scheduled for a non-stress test at the doctor's office. I didn't move, therefore, they couldn't acquire any diagnostic information. So, they sent my mom to the Oak Hill Hospital in Joplin, Missouri, for an IV to begin contractions. Unaware of my mom's hidden concerns and unaware of my physical defect, the doctor was still able to see that my heart was under an immense amount of stress during the contractions and felt that a C-section would be necessary for the delivery. Although my heart was under stress, there were still no warning signs of the trauma that awaited.

On Monday, October 17, 1988, at 6:36 pm, as with the birth of any newborn child, a miracle occurred and I was born into this world.

When I was first brought forth out of the womb, the doctors knew that there was something seriously wrong with me which perplexed the doctors, because my appearance and my size were normal. However, I was not breathing or crying and had no muscle tone. It was as if I were nothing more than a little rag doll. Frantically, the pediatrician worked on me trying to get my breathing started and to get me stable as my mom watched helplessly from the operating table.

Knowing the rest of my family anxiously awaited news from the delivery room, my dad reluctantly had to leave my mom to relay the message that there were complications with the delivery and a possibility that I would have to leave my momma and be sent by helicopter to Springfield, Missouri. Immediately, my family began to pray and seek God on my behalf. It is only by His grace and mercy that I began to breathe on my own shortly after birth, because physically there was no medical explanation how I could have survived.

I was kept in the nursery overnight for observation. It was early the next morning when I was finally placed in my mother's arms for the first time. My momma said, "At that moment, when I looked upon the precious face of my motionless baby boy, I realized I must give my heart to Jesus

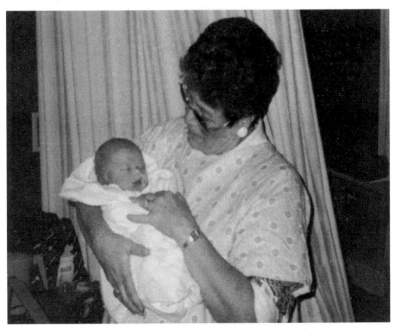

Nanny Mercer holding Baby Jacob (2 days old)

Christ and live for Him." Again, my mother kept these thoughts inside herself.

I had a little tube that was placed down my nose to my stomach to feed me, because I did not have the strength to suck from a bottle. I had never opened my eyes, because again that takes muscles and strength, but it didn't matter to my daddy, he was the proudest daddy in the whole world saying to everybody who thought I was "pretty" that "boys are not pretty, they are handsome."

Although I had never opened my eyes or been able to sufficiently intake even one ounce of formula by mouth, the pediatrician removed the nasal feeding tube from my nose and routinely, I was sent home at 4 days old with no medical changes from my birth. My parents and grandparents tried everything to get me to eat, but still no results. My mom called the pediatrician. She was told that I would eat when I got hungry. My family wanted to believe the pediatricians so bad, convincing themselves everything was all right. For 2 more days, they tried day and night to get even one ounce of food in my little body.

At 8 days old, I was placed back in the Joplin hospital where once again the tube was placed back through my nose to my stomach. Even though I was receiving nutrition now, I showed no signs of improvement. Now, when I was being fed through the tube, I would have diaphoretic sweats. My mom kept asking the nurse why I was doing this, but the doctors and nurses were baffled and had no explanation. My body began to reject the feedings. Not only was I sweating, but now, even though I know this sounds gross, had projectile vomit.

At this point, my family insisted that I be transferred to a hospital where I could get the proper medical care that I needed and, hopefully, find some answers.

When I was 11 days old and still miraculously breathing on my own, I was transferred by ambulance to the St. Francis Hospital in Tulsa, Oklahoma. There is no explanation in this world why I survived those 11 days. All I know is that God surely must have laid his hand on me and kept me alive.

3

God's Plan Beginning to Unfold

When I first arrived at the "Big Pink Hospital," St. Francis Hospital in Tulsa, Oklahoma, I became a human pin cushion. I was poked, run through machines, and placed in an oxygen bubble as doctors began to search for any explanation as to why my body was slowly, but surely shutting down.

Immediately after the test results, I was placed in the Pediatric Intensive Care Unit and my mom and dad were taken to a little conference room. My grandpa and nanny lingered at the door and amazingly were not asked to leave.

After eleven long days and just ten minutes after I was in intensive care, my little weary body slowly failed and I quit breathing. My grandpa and nanny helplessly looked on as the doctors and nurses worked frantically trying to revive me. The doctors did everything they could, but to no avail. One of the nurses said, "We have nothing," and she began to weep as she slowly turned away. In that very moment, when it seemed like all hope was gone, Jesus stepped into the picture. One male nurse stayed and shook me one final time and shouted, "Hey, wait, I've got something."

Unaware of the events taking place down the hall, my mom and dad were anxiously waiting for a report from the doctor. During this restless time, my dad, holding my mother's hand, not knowing her heart, looked at her and said, "I don't know about you, but I know what I need to do, I need to give my heart to God." My mother, with tears in her eyes, replied, "I already have." They knelt down in the room together and began to weep and pray, repenting of their sins. The very moment that my mom and dad gave their heart to Jesus, Jesus gave their baby boy back to them.

During the aftermath of the traumatizing events, at eleven days old, now I not only had a feeding tube through my nose, because I could not eat on my own, I was also placed on life support, because I could no longer breathe on my own. Despite the fact that life had returned to my body, the doctors gave no hope to my family. They were told I would never go home as long as I was on life support.

Even though the doctors gave my family no hope, my family knew whom their hope was founded in and that was in Jesus Christ. They believed in a God that could work miracles.

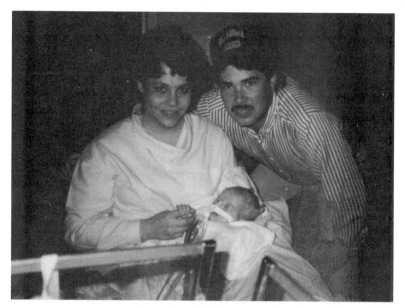

Baby Jacob and Mom & Dad at the "Pink Hospital"

Days turned into weeks and weeks turned into months. During these long days and weeks, there were many family members, church family, friends, and even strangers who God sent my family's way to give them strength and encouragement. Thanksgiving came and went as they continued to run blood tests, neurological tests, muscle, skin and nerve biopsies trying to diagnose the cause of my physical defect, but still no specific answer, although, on top of every thing else, I was diagnosed with an enlarged heart and was prescribed needed medications to slow my heart rate.

My condition remained stable, but unchanged. I still had no strength to breathe or eat on my own. It was determined that I would need a permanent tracheotomy and gastrostomy tube for which surgery was performed when I was two months old. As Christmas approached, the likelihood of my

19

ever going home did not look very promising. The doctor's words kept running through my mother's head, "He will never go home as long as he is on life support." However, my mom had determined in her heart that she would not leave the hospital and go home without her son.

Seeing the determination of my mother and father, the doctors attempted to wean me off the ventilator. At one point there was a glimmer of hope that I might come off the ventilator and go home.

There was excitement and joy as preparations were made to send me home; only to be followed by disappointment as I struggled to breathe as I lay in my mother's arms and my heart rate rapidly dropped. I was quickly taken from my mother's arms by the doctor and she and my dad were once again ushered out of the room.

When my parents were permitted back in the room, I was back on the ventilator never to come off again. The glimmer of hope began to grow dim. My dad had to return to work in Arkansas, but my mother stayed behind.

The doctors took counsel amongst one another and came to a conclusion. The neurologist took my mom into a room to give her an update on my condition. He could only give my mom a probable diagnosis of Leigh's Disease and only two years to live at the most. He said that I was unresponsive and gave my family the option to take me off the ventilator and let me die saying that maybe the doctors had intervened with God. My mom's immediate response was "NO! You don't love him like I love him and you don't see what I see."

My mom was not seeing with her physical eyes, but was seeing as the Lord sees — she saw my heart.

All that night my mom wrestled with what the doctor said, "Maybe we have intervened with God." The next morning she found the doctor and he was lunch meat. She quickly reminded him of who he was and who God was, telling him, "I don't know who you think you are or any of the other doctors are, but if God didn't want Jacob here he wouldn't be here today no matter what."

With that said, the doctors began to research other options. They found another boy that was on a ventilator that was living in the comforts of his own home. He had been released from a hospital in Oklahoma City, Oklahoma. This was the beginning of a new trend, patients being sent home on ventilators.

The doctors began to wonder if this could be a possibility for me. They definitely did not recommend it and, if my parents decided to take me home, they were required to sign a paper saying that they could shorten my life expectancy of only two years if I was removed from intensive care. The decision was final, I was going home.

It was the dawning of a new year, 1989, and preparations were being made for me to go home. My family had to undergo immense training. They learned infant CPR, sterile suction technique, chest percussion, ventilator functions and mechanics, how to change my tracheostomy and feeding tube and the most important phone number, 911, and Life Flight which were placed on speed dial. They basically packed the training of a respiratory therapist and nurse down in two weeks.

The doctors and staff wanted to not only make sure that my family could take care of my physical needs, but they also felt it necessary that my mom and dad receive counseling so they could be prepared mentally for the challenges that lay ahead. They recommended that my mom and dad visit with the counselor for one week.

The first day of counseling was tense. The counselor told my mom and dad that they were not accepting the fact that I could die prematurely. This upset my dad and he tried to explain their faith in Christ. The counselor commended their faith in God; however, he felt they weren't being realistic. My mom interrupted the debate and looked the counselor right in the eyes and said, "You could die tomorrow, I could die tomorrow, none of us are guaranteed tomorrow; therefore, we choose to live one day at a time and love Jacob for what he can do that day and never look at what he cannot do."

Needless to say, their first day of counseling was their last.

Back at home, there were also preparations being made. It was like extreme home makeover. There needed to be changes made from gas to electric to make a safer environment for all the oxygen and equipment that I would need. There were many family members and friends that sacrificed countless hours on this project.

With all the training, counseling, arrangements, and paper work completed and after much fervent prayer, the date was set for me to leave the hospital.

The doctors still didn't have a certain diagnosis. Their assessment was that I only had fleeting type movements in my extremities that made me appear as a little puppet. They concluded that I did not appear to recognize anyone and appeared to have very little in the way of responsiveness. They still believed that death was surely inevitable within two years or less and recommended that my mom and dad sign a written consent for an autopsy.

My family, believing in the words of Jesus Christ which says that, "I have come to give you life and give it more abundantly," refused to sign the consent.

What the doctors said was impossible was made possible. I was going to be the first patient ever dismissed from the St. Francis Hospital in Tulsa, Oklahoma that was on life support. However, my family had to follow certain conditions. First, the document stating that my life expectancy could be shortened had to be signed. Second, my family had to agree to have twenty-four hour nursing care the first day I was to be home and twelve hours the following day.

Of course, all the home medical equipment, supplies and services had to be in place, and they had to find a doctor in our small town to oversee my care. Dr. Clark Osborn agreed to that task and today says that it was the strangest phone call he had ever received in his medical career. The call from the hospital went like this: "We have this baby whose condition is stable, however, he is on life support and we

CONSENT

We, the undersigned, are the natural parents of Jacob Berry, who was born on October 17, 1988, in Joplin, Missouri, and was subsequently transferred from Missouri Hospital to Saint Francis Hospital, hereinafter referred to as "HOSPITAL", for evaluation by Hospital Physicians for severe hypotonia, which Jacob was noted at birth.

We herein acknowledge that due to our child's medical condition, he has required intubation since the day of admission to Hospital and still remains ventilator dependent to this date.

We further acknowledge that we have been advised by the physicians at Hospital that our son has what is known as Leighs disease which disease causes progressive deterioration of the central nervous system and muscular functions and which disease is invariably fatal regardless of the type of care or where said care is administered. We also understand that while it would be in the best interest that our son remain in the Pediatric Intensive Care Unit (PICU) of Hospital even though his life span expectation in all likelihood will not increase, it is still our desire to take our son home to live even though we have been advised that by removing him from the PICU of the Hospital to our home may facilitate his passing away sooner than if he was to remain in PICU at Hospital.

24

We further acknowledge that even though we have received adequate training from physicians and hospital personnel in the use of the Home Healthcare equipment and emergency resuscitating equipment that our home equipment will not be equal to the treatment that our son could receive in the Hospital.

Therefore, in consideration of Hospital and physicians cooperating in the removal of our son from the Hospital Intensive Care environment to our home care as we have requested, we therefore agree to assume all liability for our son's medical condition and to hold the Hospital and the physician and their respective employees, officers and agents harmless from and against any and all liabilities, losses, damages, claims, of any kind and nature as a result of their agreement to our actions as hereinabove set forth.

Dated this 25th day of _January_, 1989.

Kristine M. Schueren RN
Witness

Yvonne Berry
Yvonne Berry

Kristine M. Schueren RN
Witness

Joe Berry
Joe Berry

don't know what is wrong with him. Would you be willing to oversee his care?"

May I add right here that Dr. Osborn and all the doctors and medical personnel in my little town have done a tremendous job taking care of me and have always been a help and support to my family.

And, last but not least, if I were to leave the hospital and go home, I had to be transported by ambulance.

Finally, the monumental day had arrived, January 26, 1989. My momma combed my hair and got me all dressed up for my homecoming day. The nurses, doctors, respiratory therapists, physical therapists, and other personnel that we had drawn so close to in the past three months, made their way to my room and with tear-filled eyes, said their goodbyes and wished my family and me the best.

After all the emotional farewells and every check list checked and rechecked, they wheeled me on the cot with all my equipment to the ambulance. It was actually happening, after three long, agonizing months, I was going home, ventilator and all.

As the ambulance pulled away from the hospital, it was the beginning of a new life, a life that I could never imagine.

4

Showing Signs of Improvement

Words cannot express the feeling of joy that swept over my family as the ambulance pulled up to my little yellow house on "G" Street Northwest in Miami, Oklahoma, where a marquee sign with big bold lettering said, "Welcome Home Baby Jacob" set on the front lawn and gathered around it were a host of family and friends to witness this miracle.

As they lifted me out of the ambulance and wheeled me into the house, the respiratory therapist, the nurse and the EMT hovered over me as I was transferred to my very own baby bed. They monitored my vital signs making sure that I had made the trip home without any major complications. They inspected my ventilator and other equipment to confirm everything was in working order. I was doing fine and my equipment was working properly, so, I was left in the hands of my family and the nurse that was required to be there. I was beginning to settle in to my new environment and my family was settling in with me. That evening my grandparents stayed and my Uncle Randy, Aunt Donna, and my cousins MaRanda and Natasha came over. My Aunt Donna had cooked vegetable soup and brought it for supper. As bedtime drew near, a new nurse came for the night shift. Everyone went home and my mom and dad went to bed to get a good night's rest and left me in the care of the nurse.

The following day, my mother would finally get to be my mom and take care of me. My father would finally get to be my daddy and play with me and act silly without anybody watching him and thinking he was crazy. There were still visits from the nurse and respiratory therapist that day that reassured my parents. Family and friends were in and out. The day passed quickly and it wasn't long before the night nurse returned for one final time.

It was official ... I had lived one day at home and survived.

From the next morning forward, my mom, my dad, my grandpa and my nanny shared in the responsibility of taking care of me and all my medical needs. Every four hours I had to have chest percussion, be suctioned and fed. This whole process took about two hours then it would all start over again.

My family quickly got into a routine. My dad had to travel for his job to keep insurance for me, so when he was on the road, my grandpa and nanny would move in with me and help my momma. When my daddy would come home, they would move back to their house and my daddy would help my momma. Everyone had their turn and time for my care.

It was during one of the 10 pm feedings when my mom was sitting in the rocking chair waiting the thirty minutes before she could finish feeding me, she glanced over to my baby bed and saw Jesus standing over my bed. She didn't see His face, but she saw Him from His side in His long light blue flowing robe as He reached His hands out and touched my little body and head. She turned her head and as quickly as He was in her sight, He was gone.

At first she was afraid that Jesus had come to take me to my home in Heaven and she wasn't ready to let me go. Then Jesus revealed to her that no matter what obstacles lay ahead, her baby boy, I, was truly in His hands.

It was only because of the Lord's help that I began to slowly, but surely improve. Every little thing that I did or accomplished was a milestone and a miracle from God. Though the doctors thought I was unresponsive, my family knew in their heart that this wasn't true. I proved that when my nanny handed me a little toy that was white on one side and had a little yellow duck on the other side. She put the toy in my little chubby hand with the white side facing me.

With much effort, I would work to turn the toy around so that I could see the duck. Not only would I turn the duck facing me, but I would turn the duck right side up. There was something in my head that worked after all.

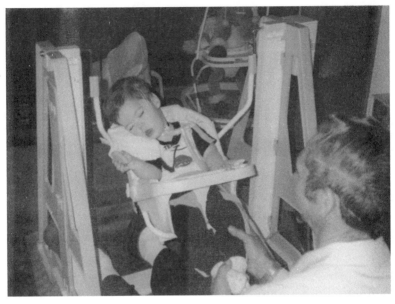

Grandpa swinging Jacob to sleep.

I began to increase in stature, but very little in strength. I didn't like sitting up much and since I couldn't cry out loud, I would make awful faces and tears would run down my face when my momma sat me in my swing for the first few times. After a few weeks, my swing became my favorite place to be; so much so that the automatic button wore out. So, for countless hours, my grandpa would sit in the living room floor and swing me in my swing until I would fall asleep.

My family decided that I was not going to lay all my life, but that I was going to get up and start moving. I not only began physical therapy and speech therapy three days a week, but a teacher also came to my house once a week.

My early days in physical therapy with Carla were not my favorite, because she would work me over good. However, she did everything she could to make it fun. Even when I was a little older and loved Popeye, she would pretend to string up an IV of spinach so I would quit pretending to pop open a can and eat it every time she would ask me to move a muscle with effort.

I did look forward to my teacher, Barbara, coming over because I thought she was just somebody else to play with. She would bring over cool toys that I never realized were educational.

I had several different speech therapists when I was a baby. Since I didn't have the strength to vocalize, I was taught sign language, mostly by my momma, and reinforced by my speech therapist and Barbara, which I picked up on pretty quickly. I was signing well over three hundred words by the time I was two.

L - Natasha R - MaRanda, at Jacob's 2nd Birthday Party

During the day, I would spend my time in the living room in my swing or on an egg crate pallet on the floor. My two cousins, MaRanda and Natasha, who are practically like sisters to me, would spend their summer days out of school with us. They would argue amongst themselves whose turn it was to hold me or feed me. They would constantly sit in the floor in front of me and sit me up in their lap. They would play with me and move my arms and legs around. I was like their little rag doll.

Sometimes my mom would be forced to make them lay me down so my food could settle in my stomach. Some of my fondest memories were watching MaRanda and Natasha, mostly Natasha, make complete fools of themselves entertaining me.

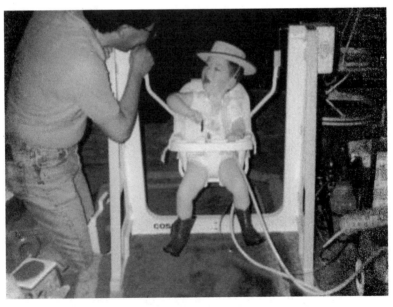

My Dad and I playing cowboys and Indians.

I was never left lying alone. Somebody was always sitting with me and keeping me entertained. Since I couldn't get up and play like any normal baby, they brought the fun to me.

My dad loved playing cowboys and Indians with me like all fathers and sons like to do. He bought me every kind of toy gun imaginable. My favorite gun was my little yellow water gun. My daddy always tried to get me to play with the fancy toy guns, but I would be insistent that I wanted my yellow gun. It was small enough and light weight enough for my little weak muscles to hold on to.

I was quite the cowboy sitting in my swing hanging on to my big stuffed horse sporting my red cowboy boots, my goofy looking cowboy hat with a bright red star on the front and whistle on the string, and my yellow water pistol. Whenever my dad would holler, "Stick 'em up," even though I was weak, I would stick my little hands in the air as far as I could reach. Then daddy would holler, "Bang, Bang," as if to shoot me; and I would die a dramatic death. Then the whole scenario would start all over again.

Everyone in the family had their own unique way of entertaining me. My Grandma Berry came from Grove to see me and play with me about once a week. Grandpa Mercer would strum on his guitar and sing to me. As I got a little older, we would build with Lincoln logs just so that I could knock them over. Nanny Mercer would sing me nursery rhymes.

My momma, well, she didn't know how to play "boy" games; when she played with me, she always tried to incorporate some kind of learning activity or strengthening game. Everyday she would come up with inventive ways to teach me different things. She continued teaching me sign language, but when I had gained enough strength to begin to make slight noises, she immediately went to work on teaching me how to say, "mama."

On March 20, 1990, at fifteen months old, I spoke my first word, "mama." It was a miracle, another gift from God, my momma, who thought she would never hear her son's voice, heard him speak her name.

I continued using sign language as my main source of communication because vocalizing and articulating was difficult. However, that just added to the list of things to work on. Sometimes my mom was glad people could not understand me.

One day, my mom, my nanny, MaRanda, and Natasha decided to take me outside in the stroller for a walk. My nanny pushed me while my momma bagged me (breathed for me with a manual resuscitator). I saw a little elderly lady outside working in her yard. She wore a big straw hat that tied under her chin with a big scarf, big sunglasses, and garden gloves. She came out to the street to greet me. I, being new to the outside world, signed to my momma, "Clown, momma."

I always wanted my mom to interpret what I had signed so I would know she understood me. Well this is one time, she improvised and said, "Yes, Jacob, that is a nice lady."

I became a little indignant because I thought my mom didn't understand me. So I signed again, "No, momma, CLOWN!"

Again, my mom refused to interpret and we told the nice lady goodbye and headed down the street. That was probably just as well.

My mom would also do different things to improve my strength. I loved watching Sesame Street. So, during the time that I watched Sesame Street on television, instead of letting me lay on the floor and watch it, for one hour, she would prop me up in the floor, and give me some support, praying that one day, I would have the strength to sit up by myself.

Six days before my second birthday on October 11, 1990, her prayers were answered and I sat up unsupported in the floor all by myself.

My family adjusted to a new way of living and life went on. Even though I had been dismissed from the hospital, everyday brought new challenges. Transporting me was very difficult. However, this would not keep my family from taking me to church. It was arranged that I would be taken to my church, First Free Will Baptist of Miami, Oklahoma, for the very first time on Easter Sunday morning March 26, 1989 and dedicated to the Lord.

Complications arose and like all my other first holidays, I spent my first Easter in the hospital instead of at church.

Jacob's Dedication to the Lord and First Trip to Church

My dedication was rescheduled and on April 9, 1989, when I was five and a half months old, I made my first trip to church. We had a large oxygen bottle set up in the choir room, along with a little foam pallet to lay me on in case I needed suctioned. We brought my ventilator in my little red wagon. Then my mom carried me in her arms and bagged me until I could be placed on my ventilator. It was all worth the effort, for, on that day, my mom and dad, and family officially dedicated me to the Lord.

There were many close calls during the first two years at home and two trips back to the hospital by life flight. The first being Easter and the second was on my mom's first Mother's Day. The day began as normal on a Sunday morning at church, which is the only place I had ever been besides home and the hospital, so my family decided to venture out a little further and that afternoon, they loaded up all my equipment and took me to my Uncle Randy and Aunt Donna's house. I seemed to tolerate the day just fine.

That evening, my dad and grandpa went back to church while my mom and nanny stayed home with me. Thirty short minutes later, my mom tried to wake me up and could not get a response. I was at the point of near death, again. My nanny called 911 and then called the church, as my mom frantically tried to awake me. Shortly after the ambulance arrived, my church family arrived. One EMT was on the phone with the Pediatric Intensive Care doctor out of Tulsa while the other assisted my mom. The intensive care doctor told the EMT there was no medication that they could give me to help me and they would send life flight. I needed another miracle.

In the meantime, the church folks had gathered in my kitchen, forming a prayer circle. One of my cousins, Sandy, my Grandpa's niece, shared with my mom a few months later that as they prayed, she saw a vision of an angel standing in the center of their prayer circle listening to their prayers. She said he then walked into the living room where I lay lifelessly, and gently kneeled down and touched my head.

I had to be transported by life flight to Tulsa. My mom flew with me. My dad, grandpa and nanny gathered things up and drove down. But before they left, my grandpa went back into the house to grab one more thing to take to the hospital, there was a silence in my room, no equipment running and there in my baby bed lay my favorite toy, my Raggedy Andy, that I had gotten for my very first Christmas.

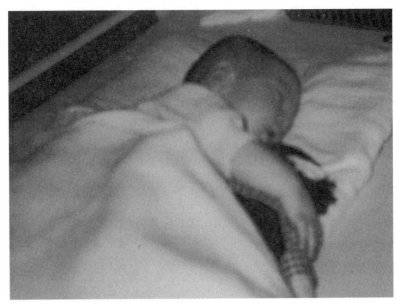

Baby Jacob sleeping with Ragedy Andy

In the emptiness and silence of my room, grandpa could not hold back the tears as he grabbed my Raggedy Andy and headed to the hospital. By the very next day, prayers had been answered, life was once again restored to my body and I was sent back home.

When we arrived back home, my family found that not only had our church family been praying, but we found a message on our answering machine from my cousin Natasha who was eight years old at the time, sobbing and praying and pouring her little heart out to God for me to be well.

Life returned to normal, well, normal for us.

People would visit from time to time. One in particular that came almost every day was one of my mom's best friends, Liz. During the weekdays she would come over after work and have supper with us. She took my mom's deposits to the bank and mailed her bills. But, what I remember most about her is that she, also, spoiled me rotten. She would bring me every Sesame Street toy, movie, and even Sesame Street Christmas ornaments.

Mom tells me that she bought me a lot of cute clothes, too, but, as any kid, I liked the toys best. My mom didn't leave the house much, because of me. So, she always looked forward to Liz coming over. Liz has always been there any time we needed her.

There have been others who have helped in time of need, whether the need be great or small. I didn't leave the house to go anywhere except church. If I did, it was a major ordeal and lots of planning beforehand. Well, it came to the point where I was in dire need of my first haircut. It was six days before my first birthday and, according to my mom, I had to look perfect for this big occasion. After all, it was another miracle in my life.

The dilemma was how to accomplish this simple and ordinary task to others, but for us a challenging predicament. Just so happens that my nanny's hairdresser, Blossom, also faced some of the same challenges with her child that we faced. So, she understood what we were going through and she offered to come to my house for my first hair cut. Even though that challenge was met, Blossom still had the challenge of cutting my hair and keeping me still, because I was not happy at all about my first hair cut.

Now that I looked perfect, it was time to celebrate my first birthday. It was a birthday that had not been taken for granted, but one cherished for the miracle that it was. We had a houseful of family and friends that joined in this cele-bration. My grandpa and nanny say that my mom and dad bought me the whole toy store. I was overwhelmed with all the festivities, but my parents were overwhelmed that this day had come.

5

A New Heart

After the celebration of my first birthday, we continued to live our lives one day at a time not taking one moment for granted, but making every moment count. However, because I had overcome so many near-death experiences and now had begun to gain more in strength and health in my body, my parents were able to begin making plans for a future beyond that single day.

They looked for different seating options besides my favorite swing. I got a walker, high chair, even though I couldn't eat out of it, a rocking chair, a cookie monster bean bag, you name it, they tried every chair imaginable to sit me up. My grandpa built different heights of little tables for me to play on while I sat in each different chair.

Even though transporting was still difficult, we started attending church every Sunday morning. Our church was only a short distance from our house so my mom would just bag me on the trip. On nice days when we would get home, dad would put my ventilator, it could run for about 20 minutes on internal battery, in my little red wagon, then mom would set me in the wagon and hold me up and grandpa would pull me down the street a little ways.

My family eventually purchased a salvaged van and a friend helped rebuild it. They built a platform on the back to hold a generator, because at that time my equipment could only be powered by electric. This van allowed us to get out of the house a little more. Sometimes, my dad and mom and I would just go out for rides. When we would stop to visit people, they would come to the van because I still required the electric for my ventilator. The only way I could get out was in my stroller and my mom would bag me, which she did for two hours on my very first trip to Toys 'R Us.

Things started looking up for me. My mom started noticing that my heart rate had stopped increasing dramatically when I was being fed as in times past and when I slept it began to drop to a more normal rate. In times past, my heart rate would sometimes increase to 180 - 200 beats per minute.

My family had always worried about my heart after my diagnosis of a cardiomyopathy, an enlarged heart. They were concerned that my little heart would eventually give out under so much stress. So, from the first moment I was diagnosed as a baby, they began to pray that God would give me a miracle for my heart.

My Great, Great Aunt Violet had a bad heart also. She would always come up to me and pat my little hand and say, "This is your old Aunt Violet." My Aunt Violet was a praying Christian woman. She always prayed for the Lord to take her life and give me life.

It came to pass, on September 10, 1990 that Aunt Violet went home to be with the Lord and received a new body and new heart in Heaven. I can just picture Aunt Violet seeing Jesus face to face and saying on my behalf, "Lord, see little Jacob, he needs a new heart."

One month before my second birthday and eight days after Aunt Violet's passing, on September 18, 1990, I had an appointment at St. Francis Hospital in Tulsa, Oklahoma, to have an echo cardiogram to check my heart. The technician began the procedure. He started comparing what he was seeing on the screen to my previous record of my echo cardiogram in my chart. In a confused voice, he asked my parents, "Is this Jacob Berry?"

My parents told him, "Yes."

He then asked, "Is this Jacob KEITH Berry?"

My parents said, "Yes."

The technician, astonished, said in amazement, "This boy has a brand new heart." I no longer had to take any heart medication. God had answered the prayers of my family and my Aunt Violet.

When I think about what God did for me, I think of when the Psalmist David said, "Create in me a clean heart, O God." I believe God not only gave me a brand new physical heart that day, but He also gave me a heart that would love Him and as David, that I would become a man that would seek after God's own heart.

6

The Miracle
That Keeps on
Going

My early childhood is something that I vaguely remember, but something that my parents will never forget. Since I couldn't walk and explore the big world around me, I explored my world and learned from watching the television. I can recall lying on my blanket in the floor and watching the Disney classics, "Peter Pan" and "The Jungle Book."

The hours that I wasn't watching TV, I would sit up in one of my chairs with a table and play with puzzles, puppets and toys. I was always fascinated with building blocks, just so that I could knock them down. Since I couldn't move around, somebody was always sitting with me and entertaining me. The ironic thing is, I would be the one entertaining them.

Everyday was like this until the day I got my first set of wheels. It was nothing more than a simple push chair, but it had a vent tray. It was a used chair and a little worn. I was now officially mobile, or so I thought. My first tour was through my own house, then on to the great outdoors.

My family pushed me everywhere and I had no problem telling them where to push me. This wheelchair was only

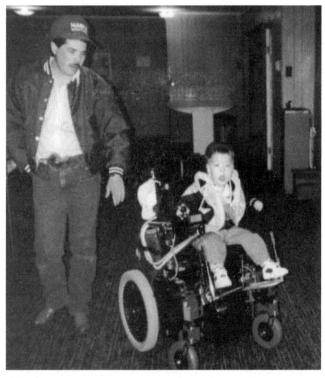

Learning How to Drive at Age 2

46

temporary, though. I was getting ready to climb to new heights.

I was only two years and five months old when I was OFFI-CIALLY mobile, set free, and dangerous in my first motor-ized, power wheelchair, a 1990 Red Invacare Jaguar model.

It was a cold evening when we arrived back home with my chair. God, through Children's Miracle Network, had provided a van lift for me so that my new chair with me in it could be transported. My house at the time was too small for an inexperienced driver in such a big chair. So, my first test drive was in the fellowship hall of our church. The only maneuver I could achieve was a circle, but it didn't matter as I happily went round and round experiencing my new found freedom.

The next day I was taken to the park for more driving lessons. It didn't take me long to figure out how to stop going in circles and start driving straight.

Learning how to drive was like a baby learning to walk, small and slow steps at first. Slow being the key word for someone learning to drive a chair. My parents didn't teach me how to put my chair in high gear until I was older, espe-cially when I was in the house or church. Same rule applied "no running in the church house" or, for me, "no driving fast."

As all little boys learning to walk begin to get into mischief, so did I. My Grandpa and I would lock my mom in the windowless laundry room and turn out the light. It wasn't that there was a lock on the door, but I would shut the door with my foot and put my powerful wheelchair against the door. When my chair was in gear, it could not be pushed or moved. I thought this was a funny game and so did everybody else until the day when no one was home except me and my mom. I was still only two and should I come off my ventilator or need suctioned someone needed to be right there with me.

This particular day, I was in my wheelchair in the kitchen watching my mom put clothes in the dryer when I got bored and decided to play our little game. I manipulated my chair around quickly, and before she could react, I had locked my mom in the laundry room. She had a small crack in the door where she could see me. I crawled my little, chubby hand up the wall to turn off the light. My mom began to panic in the pitch, black darkness as she contemplated to herself, "What if he needs suctioned or worse and I can't get to him."

She kept telling me I needed to move and let momma out, but she could see through the small crack in the door me shaking my head "no." After about ten minutes, she knew she wasn't going to out-will me at this point, so she decided to out smart me and told me to go look and see if Grandpa was coming home for lunch. It worked and I drove to the patio door to see if I could see Grandpa. My momma never went in the laundry room again when we were alone in the house.

Now that I had all this new freedom, mobility, and energy, my parents wanted to take me everywhere. They wanted me to experience this wonderful gift called life to the fullest.

7

Childhood Journeys

My first overnight trip was, of all places, Tulsa, Oklahoma. However, this time it was a good overnight trip because I was not going back to the "pink hospital' but to a motel, the zoo, Chuck E. Cheese and Toy's R Us.

Every time we went on an overnight trip, we had to pack like we were moving to a new house. My dad was the one who had to load and unload the van. Sometimes I felt sorry for him because he had to do all the work, but if you ask him today, he would say it was worth it just to see me smile.

One of my favorite places to go in the summer was ventilator camp in Guthrie, Oklahoma. Ventilator camp was a special summer camp designed specifically for children on ventilators and their entire family. It was a chance for us kids to be "normal," not having people stop and stare.

Of course, I was only 2 years old the first time I went to camp and I was the one that was doing all the staring, because for the first time in my life, I saw kids that looked like me. I kept signing to my momma, "Momma, vent like me."

Those days sure were fun, nothing but fishing, riding on a paddle boat, swimming, and playing. One of the funniest memories that I have was the last year that they had vent camp, it rained and rained, so no fishing, paddle boats, or swimming — just hanging out and being boys playing Sega genesis.

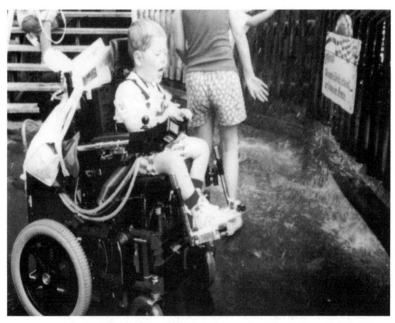

Jacob (age 2) enjoying the log ride (his own way)
at Silver Dollar City

This camping trip was also helpful to the parents as they shared different ways and ideas to help their children with simple everyday life.

Another place I liked going during the summer was with my cousins, Natasha and MaRanda, to the creek. Looking back, my mom cringes at the thought of putting her fragile, handicapped child in dirty, nasty creek water. But, at the time she just wanted me to experience life to the fullest and what is a childhood without swimming in the creek.

I can remember one particular summer, my family and I went to Silver Dollar City, the most popular theme park in the Ozark Mountains. It was extremely hot the day we went, so my favorite spot in the whole park was by the log ride where you were sure to get soaked with cold water every time the boat would plunge into the water. Even though I couldn't ride the log ride, I found my own special way to enjoy it.

All these vacations were fun and wonderful, but my favorite of all came when I was four years old. Through the generosity of the Make A Wish Foundation, I got the opportunity to go to Walt Disney World in Orlando, Florida. Although I had become a seasoned traveler, I had only been three hours from home on any trip. A three-day trip, well that was a whole new experience.

My cousins, Darrell and Sandy Williams, loaned my Grandpa and Nanny their mini van and took the back seats out so they could follow us to transport all my equipment, food and supplies that I would need for this trip. Even though my dad had fixed up our van so I could watch movies during the trip, I think I still drove my parents crazy asking them every hour, "Are we there yet?"

Three days later, we finally arrived!

We stayed at a special resort called Give Kids the World where children with all types of life threatening diseases were privileged to stay with their families. We had tickets for three days at any Walt Disney World Park. Since I was so young and couldn't tolerate long, hot days, we spent all three days at the Magic Kingdom so that I could see and do everything that I desired.

Jacob meeting his favorite Disney character

We spent most of the first day looking for Donald Duck, my favorite Disney character. Once that formal introduction had been made, we could now explore the rest of the park.

Of all the things that we did, my favorite was the night time parade. Maybe that's because of the special treatment that I not only received then, but throughout the entire time I was there.

I can honestly say that Walt Disney World truly goes out of their way and knows how to make a child with special needs dreams come true.

When we really stop and think about it, that is how we as Christians should treat all people. We need to treat them as if they are something special, because in God's eyes we are all special.

So as you can see, I became an outgoing child in my youth, always having fun. I never met a stranger, even though many people that encountered me thought I was a little strange.

I loved going on trips and meeting new people. No matter where I went or how many people I talked to, the Lord Jesus Christ would always be mentioned in the conversation whether initiated by me or them. I guess in some ways, even in my youth, God was beginning to mold me into a Miracle on a Mission.

Of all my childhood journeys, the most life-changing journeys were my trips every Sunday to the little gray church on the corner of Main Street, for it was there that I first heard of a land with no more wheelchairs. This land called Beulah land is the place that I long to see and some day will be my final journey.

That will be the most amazing trip ever!

8

Church Days

I grew up in the First Free Will Baptist Church of Miami, Oklahoma. It was a small church with many precious memories. Every Sunday morning we would get up early so momma could get me ready for Sunday School and church.

My first memories of church were that of Sunday School class and my first Sunday School teacher, Sister Shirley Reece. The Bible stories would always seem to come to life as Sister Shirley would tell the stories and use the old fashion flannel graph pictures.

My favorite Old Testament story was that of David and Goliath. However, that story almost got me and grandpa in trouble one day at home. We were playing David and Goliath. Grandpa was David and I was the mighty giant Goliath. As I ran at Grandpa in my wheelchair pretending to be Goliath, Grandpa, now in the character of David, swung his pretend slingshot and threw the rock. I dramatically fell face forward in my chair just as Goliath had fallen mightily on his face, however, my chair did not die the dramatic death that I did. It kept right on going with me in it through the wall. When I saw what I had done, I said, "Oh, no, momma's gonna get me."

It was in Sister Shirley's class that I also learned the stories of Jesus, how He healed the sick and made the lame to walk. I remember thinking, even as a child, if this Jesus could do that for those people, then what can He do for me.

After the Sunday School bell rang, it was time for church. Still today, I can hear the old songs of Zion ringing in my ears and in my heart as the worship hour would begin. Brother Dewey Johnston was the pastor of the church during most of my childhood and the pastor that I can first remember sitting under. He was a very smart man of God with much wisdom in the Bible. He even helped me with research on a few of my school projects.

I can remember saying as a little boy, "I want to grow up and be a preacher just like Brother Dewey." I heard him preach many sermons, and at my young age, some that I couldn't understand, however, I understood this one thing: Jesus loved me.

At five years old, I also came to understand that it wasn't what Jesus could do for me, but what Jesus had already done for me. It was something much greater than raising me out of my wheelchair, but I understood that Jesus had died on the cross for my sins and rose again so I could be saved from the bondage of sin. So, it was at the age of five, that I asked Jesus to forgive me of my sins and to live in my heart.

I longed to follow in the footsteps of Jesus and be baptized by emersion. My family and I never thought that this would be possible because of my tracheostomy and ventilator dependence. I never gave up on that desire to follow Jesus, and on May 3, 1998, when I was 9 years old, with my tracheostomy capped off, I was baptized. Anything is possible with God.

I always loved going to church and learning more about Jesus, but sometimes as a little boy, I wondered why church lasted so long. It was during one of these longer services when I was seven years old that an evangelist with the gift of healing was preaching at our church. He didn't know my situation or that my family had prayed for me to be able to swallow and manage my own saliva. He came to me and said, "I don't understand it, but I see his (referring to me) throat paralyzed, but slowing and gradually over time begin-ning to work."

This miracle came to pass and I began to manage my own saliva, drink liquids and swallow small bites of soft food by the time I was 9 years old. I can still remember the tears not only in my momma's eyes when I first swallowed that bite of food, but also in my speech teacher's, Mrs. Windle's, eyes as well.

They knew they were witnessing a miracle from God.

Jacob signing at Grandma Berry's church

As a little boy, I use to sign a song in church for a special by Mary Rice Hopkins entitled, "I'm A Little Miracle." I not only signed in my home church when I was little, but on special occasions, we would travel to Grove, Oklahoma, and attend church with my Grandma Berry and there at her church I would sign, also.

God has done many miracles in my life; however, I know the greatest miracle in any life is the miracle of salvation through the blood of Jesus Christ. I thank God that I grew up in a church where the cross and the message of redemption was preached.

9

The Diagnosis of Muscular Dystrophy

The first six years of my life, I did not realize that I was different than anyone else until the day I was watching a home video of my birthday party. We were playing the cake walk game wheelchair style where you put the numbers on the ground and walk on the numbers instead of using chairs.

While viewing this, I suddenly realized that I was different than my friends. I looked at my grandpa and said, "Grandpa, I can't walk." This really tugged at my grandpa's heart and he wasn't quite sure how to respond. I wasn't upset or angry, just amazed and stating what I saw.

We are all different and unique in our own way, but that is how God created us. I have always accepted the fact that I am in a wheelchair and who I am. I know that I am not a mistake, but I am fearfully and wonderfully made. I think many people today try to be somebody that God has not created them to be and that is why there are so many unhappy people in this world today.

I never really questioned being in a wheelchair. However, one day when I was seven, my mom and I were leaving the library and I saw a young woman using a walker and struggling with every step. As a curious seven year old, I asked my mom why she couldn't walk very well. My mom explained that the young lady had a condition called cerebral palsy. Analyzing her condition and mine, I asked my mom, "Is that why I can't walk?" My mom knew I didn't have cerebral palsy, but really had no answer to my question. She explained to me about how I had never really received a specific diagnosis, only a probable diagnosis and she had her doubts about that diagnosis of Leigh's Disease.

My mom had read an article in *Exceptional Parent Magazine* in the parent search section about boys with the same symptoms that I had which had been diagnosed with X-Linked Myotubular Myopathy, a rare form of Muscular Dystrophy that is passed through the X Chromosome of the mother. In 1994, over 50% of children having myotubular myopathy died within the first two years of life. She kept this in the back of her mind and always knew that this is what I had.

Sparked by her research and curiosity, I was scheduled for an appointment with the same neurologist that had given me a probable diagnosis and basically no hope.

This doctor had not seen me for six years. Needless to say, I had made HUGE progress. I was a rambunctious seven-year-old boy in a 250-pound wheelchair.

After examining me, my mom said that he was thrilled with my improvement because he had spent many sleepless nights when I was a baby trying to figure out how to help me. Being the intelligent man that he was, he sometimes had difficulty relating his feelings. His comment about how well I was doing was, "I think this child needs to be on ritalin."

The funny thing is there were many times, as my mom sat beside me everyday in school, that she wondered the very same thing.

The possibility of my having myotubular myopathy was discussed and it was determined the next surgery that I required, we would do another muscle biopsy.

It wasn't but a few months later I had some teeth pulled, along with another minor surgery, and the muscle biopsy was done.

Sure enough, I had exactly what my mom had thought. As bad as I don't like to admit it, sometimes I do think moms know everything.

I will never forget the day the doctor called with the confirmation. My dad was gone out of town for work so my grandpa and nanny were staying with me. My nanny was in the kitchen and I hollered out at her, "Hey nan, guess what I have, I have muscular dystrophy," as if I had just won an award. Then I told grandpa, "We need to pray to Jesus and tell Him what I have so He can heal me."

Grandpa said, "Jacob, Jesus already knew what you had."

I am so glad that before we even pray, our Heavenly Father knows what we stand in need of.

10

Early School
Years

Despite having muscular dystrophy and all the challenges that come with it, I was the happiest boy alive. I started lab school, which was a program at the junior college in Miami for the students majoring in different childhood developments to spend time and observe children. I was definitely a whole new experience for the group of students who were there when I attended. It is not everyday that you encounter a three year old in a 250 pound wheelchair.

It was there in lab school that I met my first friend, Holly Goforth. Through the years, even though we each had our different friends and different interests, I feel God placed a special bond as friends between us that will continue throughout our lifetime. That feeling was confirmed and I was so humbled and honored the first time she came to hear me preach. You can never put a price on friendship. The Bible says, in Proverbs Chapter 18 verse 24:

> "A man that hath friends must shew himself friendly: and there is a friend that sticketh closer than a brother."
>
> — Proverbs 18:24 (KJV)

After two years of lab school, I was now prepared for Kindergarten, but we had to prepare Kindergarten for me. They weren't quite sure if it would be good for my social well being for my momma to be at school with me everyday.

That was the last thing my mom was worried about, my social well being. She knew I was a social butterfly. My mom only went with me for my physical well being and to assist me with my needs.

From Kindergarten through my Senior year in high school, my mom went to school with me. She is probably the only person that has gone through school twice. Sometimes it was a blessing to have my mom at school with me; other times when she made me do my work, I am not so sure.

With all the preliminaries out of the way, my first day of Kindergarten was something my mom will never forget. My first paper was a picture of a school house that I had to color. With much confidence, I proudly took my blue crayon and drew a cross on top of my school house and said, "Mine is a Jesus school house."

Jacob's 1ˢᵗ Kindergarden
Paper - He put a cross
- On top + said it was
Jesus School House.

8-17-94   6 years old

65

I don't remember Kindergarten as being anything hard with lots of work — only lots of playing and making more new friends.

It wasn't until first grade that I found out that school wasn't all fun and games. Up until first grade, I had pretty much always called the shots and done what I wanted to do whenever I wanted to do it. I was about to get a rude awakening. The first paper that I decided I didn't want to do and tossed on the floor was patiently, the first time, picked up by my mother and placed back in front of me. The second time it hit the floor not so patiently picked up by my mother and put in front of me. The third and last time it hit the floor and placed back in front of me, my momma took a pencil, placed it in my hand and showed me who was in charge and this time it wasn't me calling the shots.

It was during my early school years that my mom found out just how strong willed I really was. However, I also learned from where that trait was passed, because, my mom's strong will always won out over mine.

I was a typical boy. I was not interested in school except for recess and PE, where I got to play with my friends. When the teacher was talking, I was a million miles away in my own little world. You see, being in a wheelchair and connected to a ventilator, sometimes I couldn't physically get to where I wanted to be, but my mind and imagination could take me anywhere. I would imagine myself as a great sports figure. I would imagine myself playing baseball for the Houston Astros alongside Jeff Bagwell and Craig Biggio. Then there were days I would be catching the game winning pass from Troy Aikman for the Dallas Cowboys. My all-time favorite was playing basketball like Michael Jordan. I always dreamed of playing sports.

When I came back to reality, nothing had changed; I was still the same me and still had to do the same boring school work. But what I didn't realize at 7 years old, God was already beginning to use me for His plan for my life. Every time Mrs. Barker, my 1st grade teacher, would ask a question, I would raise my hand to answer and my answer no matter the question would have something to do with Jesus. So much so that one of the little girls in my class, Chelsey, said, "Man, he sure likes God, doesn't he."

Mrs. Barker just replied, "Yes, he does."

There were many good days in school along with a few bad which I brought on myself, but in spite of my foolish childhood behavior, Christ never left me, and I would always ask forgiveness when I acted ugly and didn't want to do my schoolwork. I can recall telling my mom several times, "Momma, I don't like school work."

Momma said, "I don't like it either."

I thought to myself, "Then, why are you making me do it?"

Being the good mother she was and teaching me responsibility, about once a week, I wound up grounded from video games or television for fussing and creating a big drama over school work. I look back now and wonder, "What was I thinking?" All I had to do was do the school work, which I had to do eventually anyway even after being grounded. Other than that, momma says that I was a pretty good kid.

Needless to say, first grade was definitely another miracle and stepping stone in my life. Looking back now, I realize that when momma was making me learn, she had the faith that I was going to live past the doctor's expectations and I would need to know how to read and write. She never gave up and said, "Well, he is in a wheelchair and not expected to live, just let him do what he wants." She never treated me any different than a normal child that could walk, because she knew that in my mind I was all there and capable of doing anything I set my mind to and by the 2nd grade I had set my mind to many things.

Second grade was an interesting year. My teacher's name was Mrs. Black who was originally from South America. She taught us English and Spanish, although I was still struggling with just speaking English. As far as school and the work, it was still same old, same old. I never listened, but this year my imagination would carry me to the wrestling ring. Back in the day when WCW was a family friendly sport, I was a full fledged Hulkamaniac. My dad even got tickets to one of the WCW events. Even though The Hulkster wasn't going to be there, we still drove five hours for this event. It was incredibly entertaining for this 7 year old.

Call me a redneck, but there isn't anything like watching two guys tear each other apart (supposedly) in the squared circle.

I saw many great wrestling matches, but there is no fight that could compare to the fights that mom and I had over school work. Therefore, occasionally, when dad was home from work, he would attend school with me until middle school, then if mom couldn't go, which wasn't often, I got to stay home. Having dad go to school with me proved to be even more stressful to my mom, because, one day in second grade, I came home with a broken leg.

You're probably thinking, "How could I break my leg when I couldn't even walk?" Well, I knocked my dad off of his feet with my wheelchair and he fell on my controller. The combination of my dad smashing my controller into my right femur, broke my leg. The funny thing is dad was the one on the floor and the one that everybody thought was hurt. I finished school that day and went to cub scouts that night. Dad and I got up the next morning and I went to school again not knowing I had a broken leg until my doctor's appointment that evening when I was congratulated for my first broken bone.

During second grade, I started reading the Marc Brown books about the aardvark, "Aurthur." I was inspired by the fact that Aurthur had his very own club. So I decided to start my own club. My club was going to be "The Jesus Club." I invited my friends over one day for a Jesus Club Meeting. We watched a Nest Entertainment Jesus movie, had snacks, made a craft, played Bible games and all received special Jesus Club bracelets (the WWJD bracelets).

Our club lasted awhile, but our meetings were short-lived because mom couldn't take a house full of second graders too many times. Reflecting back on this memory, I realize now that my "Jesus Club" was my way as a second grader of sharing Jesus. My soul's desire even at this young, tender age was to be a preacher. One of my assignments in 2nd grade was to write about what I wanted to be when I grew up and draw a picture about it. I wrote, "I want to be a preacher when I grow up to be a man, because I want to teach the world about Jesus." I drew a picture of myself behind a pulpit and a bunch of little circles for my congregation.

My ambitions to be a preacher continued on. When I was in third grade, we had a learning activity called "Third Graders Go to Work." A business in our community would open its doors to a class of third graders and demonstrate what it was like to work at that particular business. My third grade class was invited to "work" at the City of Miami. The city manager brought job applications to our classroom that we each had to fill out. There were specific job descriptions that we could choose from. I didn't read the list, but told my mom, "I want to be the city preacher."

My mom explained that was not a job that was available and there was no such thing as a city preacher. Still determined, I said, "Well, they need one."

By then everybody had finished filling out their applications and were waiting on mine. My mom, getting a little frustrated, told me to just pick a job on the list. So, reluctantly, I gave in, but with more thought, I chose to be the judge.

The next question on the application was why I thought I would be good at the job. My mom tells me that her frustration quickly faded as I told her that I wanted to be the judge, because I would pray like King Solomon for wisdom so that I could judge the people right.

2nd grade
1 month before
Jacob's
8th birthday

I want to be a Preacher
when I grow up to be a ma
Because I want to teach
the world about Jesus

We not only learned what it was like to work at the city that year, but we learned about politics. We held a third grade presidential election. If we wanted to run for president, we had to prepare a speech and come up with campaign ads. It was a heated race, but in the end I was elected and became third grade president of my class.

My mom always said that I would either be a preacher or a politician when I grew up because, I was always talking and shaking everybody's hand.

My teacher during third grade was Mrs. Buzzard. I learned a lot that year. She was a hands-on teacher which held my attention a little better. I still had my moments where I drifted into my own little world. This year I was back on the court with my favorite athlete of all time, Michael Jordan, and dreaming of playing in the NBA.

One of my favorite things to do at recess was to play basketball with my friends. One of my friends would run along side my wheelchair bouncing the ball beside me with my hand touching each time like I was dribbling down court. Then, because I didn't have enough strength to lift the ball, when I hollered, "shoot," they would shoot the basketball for me as if I was the one actually doing the shooting. When I would holler, "pass" they would pass the ball for me.

At 8 years old, I thought I was really tearing it up on the court and thinking I was really playing basketball. Therefore, one night at cub scouts when the boys were talking about signing up for city league basketball, I got the bright idea that I would go home and ask my mom if I could sign up for city league basketball. After all, I thought I could really play basketball like everybody else.

I came home that night excited and hopeful. I asked my mom, "Mom, all my friends are signing up for city league basketball, can I sign up, too?"

I can't imagine the pain that gripped my momma's heart as she had to tell me that I couldn't play city league basketball. For the first time in my life, I realized that there were some things in life that I couldn't do like everybody else. My eyes were opened that day to the fact that we are all different and unique. I thought the reason I couldn't play basketball was because of my wheelchair.

As I began to cry, my momma took me out of the wheelchair and put me in her lap and rocked me. She gently explained that even boys that could walk were not good at playing basketball and not everybody can be a basketball player. She said, "You see, God has made you to be something different than a basketball player."

Then she reminded me of what she had told the doctors when I was a baby. "We will love Jacob for what he can do today and never look at what he cannot do." So we began to list all the things that I could do that particular day.

Since that night, I have never complained about being different or being in a wheelchair. I just accept God's will for my life.

Today, many people ask me, "When did you first know that you were called to preach?" I feel like God spared my life as a baby to one day preach the gospel. Even though I didn't have a thorough understanding at a young age, God's calling was always on my life.

11

The Love
of the Game

Even though I was in a wheelchair and knew my limitations, that did not diminish my love and passion for sports, in particular, football, basketball and baseball.

I made the best of my situation and when I was young, I played "challenger league baseball, basketball, and soccer." Challenger League was a special organization set up to give kids like me and kids with all types of disabilities, whether mental or physical, the opportunity to participate in sports. With the help of our "buddies" we were able to play sports like everybody else. During the baseball season, I always wanted my jersey number to be #5 like Jeff Bagwell or #7 like Craig Biggio, both Houston Astros Legends.

Why would a guy from Miami, Oklahoma, like the Houston Astros? In the year 1997, we got the chance to go to Houston, Texas, to meet a family that had a son the same age as me with the same type of muscular dystrophy that I have.

When John and I first met, it was like looking into a mirror. His parents got us tickets to watch the Houston Astros play Barry Bonds and the San Francisco Giants in the old Astrodome. In the Astrodome, the wheelchair exit was through the player's family waiting area and also where the player's exited. There were signs that respectfully said, "No autographs, please."

I had made friends with the security and door man on the way in. He told me he would get me some souvenirs when I left. While I waited for him to get the souvenirs, being the social butterfly that I am, I introduced myself and struck up a conversation with a complete stranger who happened to be the wife of one of the Astros' players. She got a baseball, and since I couldn't ask for autographs, she did it for me and introduced me to the players as they left. I think my dad was more excited than I was. He was a big baseball fan growing up.

It was such a unique experience and I was hooked. Five more summers, we would make a trip to Houston to visit my friend John. Each year, I would go to watch the Astros play baseball and get autographs. Craig Biggio even signed the back of my Biggio T-Shirt. Although, I attended other baseball games in other stadiums and watched other teams, I became an Astros fan for life.

The year that I struggled with not being able to play basketball, since I loved Michael Jordan, my dad and mom took me to the United Center in Chicago to watch Michael Jordan play a game in his last season with the Chicago Bulls. My cousin, Natasha, got to go with us. MaRanda didn't want to go because she had a boyfriend at the time and she thought she was in love.

We sat way up in the nose bleed section and needed binoculars. It was still one of the greatest sporting experiences of my life. To me, saying that you had the opportunity to watch Michael Jordan play basketball in person is like saying you got to watch Babe Ruth play baseball in person. When Michael retired, I became a Lakers fan and even watched Kobe Bryant and Shaquille O'Neal play for the Lakers at a Dallas Mavericks game in Dallas and also a game at the Staples Center in Los Angeles, but my passion for the game of basketball has not been the same since Jordan retired.

There is one team that beats all of my favorite pro teams, the Dallas Cowboys, the Los Angeles Lakers, and the Houston Astros combined and that is the Oklahoma Sooner's Football Team (Boomer Sooner). When somebody starts talking about College Football, my ears perk up. OU has a great history and winning tradition. However, when I was a kid in the 1990s, they weren't so good. They were terrible, so it was easy to get tickets. Every season, we would make a trip to Norman, Oklahoma, to watch an OU football game, no matter how good or bad they were.

It was during half time of one of these games that they were honoring OU's 1969 Heisman Trophy Winner, Steve Owens. Steve Owens was from my hometown, Miami,

Oklahoma, and he was and still is a hometown hero. Just to think that I graduated from the same high school as a Heisman Trophy winner makes me proud to be a Miami High School Wardog. He has never forgotten his heritage as a small town boy and gives back to the community of Miami.

After we met and he found out that I was from his hometown, he has showered me with lots of priceless autographed memorabilia. Not only that, he helped me get OU tickets for me and my family.

The year that OU began winning football games and championships again, the ticket office no longer wanted to sell us three tickets in the wheelchair accessible seating, which we had bought with no problem in years past. They told us we

L - Bob Stoop, Oklahoma University Head Coach
R - Steve Owens, 1969 Heisman Trophy Winner

78

could only have one wheelchair and one attendant and either my mom or dad would have to sit in another part of the stadium. Let's just say it's great to have friends like Steve Owens. We got the three tickets that year and in future years whenever we were able to attend a game.

I just recently had the privilege of meeting Paul and Alison (Rockett) Frase, founders of the Joshua Frase Foundation, a foundation that is dedicated to the research and develop- ment for a cure for Myotubular Myopathy, my type of muscular dystrophy. The foundation is named in honor of Paul and Alison's special child Joshua who also suffered with Myotubular Myopathy, but is now running on streets of gold in Heaven.

We quickly developed a great friendship because of the many things we have in common that exceeds beyond our love for the game of football. We were sharing stories at a family conference in Minneapolis, Minnesota, when the subject of football came up. Paul, being a retired NFL player, and I had lots to talk about. Paul learned that my favorite NFL team was the Dallas Cowboys and how that when I was nine years old my parents were going to take me to a Dallas Cowboys game, but the same scenario — you can only have one wheelchair seat and one attendant.

My family of three could not attend as a family because I had Muscular Dystrophy. After debating the issue with my mom over the phone, the lady at the ticket office said to my mom, "AT LEAST your son would get to go."

That didn't set well with my prideful momma and her reply was, "My son doesn't settle for the least, we will just take him to a different event."

Paul thought that was pretty funny, because Alison's policy, Joshua's momma, was the same as my mom's, that THESE BOYS (muscular dystrophy boys) deserve the red carpet treatment and should never settle for the least. So with much collaboration between Paul & Alison and their friend, Chad Hennings, a retired Dallas Cowboy player, I got tickets to watch the 2011 Dallas Cowboys take on the St. Louis Rams at the new Cowboy's Stadium and definitely received the "Red Carpet Treatment."

Our family not only had three seats together, but our seats were in an owner's club suite with access to the exclusive owner's club and not to leave out van-accessible parking at the entrance of the stadium, only one parking space over from the player's parking. It was the greatest sporting experience of my adult life.

I have been blessed to attend and experience many sporting events and meet many sports heroes. Even though I still enjoy watching a great game, my greatest passion has and always will be Jesus Christ and preaching His gospel.

12

Herrington Rods

All of my summer vacations would start the same way. I would pray that the last day of school would hurry and get over and that the summer days would go by very slowly. As soon as the school bell rang at 3:15 pm, I was gone. Now, I could play video games, hang out with friends, and best of all, no homework.

During one of my trips to Houston during summer vacation, I went to see my friend John's back doctor. I was having trouble wearing my back brace and my scoliosis was getting worse. They made me a new brace that we thought was going to work. However, as I began my fourth grade year, I began having a lot of pain sitting up. My left rib touched my left pelvic bone. Therefore not only did my back hurt, but my hip hurt also. I would have to come home from school and go to bed which was a total bummer. I liked being up and mobile. I struggled through my fourth grade year.

Despite my struggles, it did not hinder or paralyze my walk with the Lord. I was always taught that you prayed to Jesus and talked to Him as your best friend and that you could talk to Him at any time and any where. One day, my fourth grade Social Studies teacher had the beginning of a migraine headache. After I completed my assignment, I went to hand in my paper and observed my teacher sitting in pain. I asked her what was wrong and she told me that she was getting a migraine. I reached for her hand with my little hand. She looked at my mom, puzzled.

My mom knew what I was doing and told her that I wanted to pray for her. She took my hand and during the middle of class in front of my peers, I unashamedly prayed for her. Later that day, she came to me and said, "Thank you for praying for me. My headache is gone."

I still believe in prayer and the power that it possesses.

It is only through prayer that we survived the next mountain that I faced: back surgery.

I could no longer sit up for a full day, therefore, back surgery was my last alternative. Because of the high demand for the doctor in St. Louis, Missouri, it took several months to get my surgery scheduled. My mom had hoped to get it done over the summer months so I wouldn't miss school. However, God had other plans and my surgery was scheduled for September 1, 1999.

During the summer months leading up to my surgery, my family learned of another boy my age with the same type of muscular dystrophy that I had, went through the same surgery procedure that I was facing. We were devastated and fearful when we got the news that he did not survive the procedure and went on to be with the Lord during the surgery.

As a 10-year-old, even though I knew if something were to happen to me that I was going to Heaven, this was still scary stuff. Doubts began swirling through my mind, "Will I make it or will I wake up in the arms of Jesus?" I thought to myself, "What does death taste like and would this be the last time for me to see my mother?" I tried my best to not think of these negative thoughts, as we went into the surgery pre-op preliminaries.

The day before my surgery we went to the hospital to complete the rest of the pre-op testing. We spent all day at the hospital. We went to the hospital cafeteria so my family could eat lunch. While my folks were sitting there dining, they could tell that I was not my usual talkative self. Still being nervous about the surgery and what I was facing, I began to pray.

While praying, I looked across the hospital cafeteria into a light and I could see an image of the hem of His garment walking towards me. I said, "Hey Grandpa, do you see that?" as I tried to explain to him what I was seeing. My Grandpa didn't see what I was seeing, but he had no doubts about what I saw. I knew the Lord was trying to give me strength and comfort in my hour of need. I realized that everything was going to be all right and that Jesus would be with me during my surgery. Jesus never really told me the outcome of the surgery, but he was letting me know that no matter what, I was in His powerful, unchanging hands.

September 1, 1999, my day started before the sun came up. As we pulled into the Children's Hospital in St. Louis, instead of my being the social butterfly that I usually am, my stomach had butterflies. Then came the words that I was not ready to hear, "Jacob, they are ready for you."

I can remember mom walking with me as far as she could. Since I did not want to let go of her hand, because of fear, I said to her, "I don't know if I will see you again here or not, but if not, I will see you in Heaven."

Well, that only made it worse for my mom as she clung to my hand and tried to keep a brave face, but through her tears, she told me that God knew that she needed me and she would see me after the surgery. After I finally let go of my momma's hand, I knew there was another hand, the mighty hand of Jesus, waiting to take my hand. As I went through the double doors and was wheeled into the operating room, the only thing I remember after that is my trying my best not to fall asleep.

Six agonizing hours later, I woke up in the intensive care unit and realized that God had brought me through the surgery. My head was still spinning from the anesthetic. My face was bruised and swollen from laying on it for so long and my back looked like it had been through the meat grinder and had tubes coming out of it. Even though I had a lot of recovery time ahead of me, I was alive. God was not finished with me.

The recovery process was long and difficult. Before they began anything major, you would think they would have given me a couple of days to recover. But, no, the very next day they removed the drain tubes from my back. Then, they came in and body casted me for a brace that I had to wear anytime I was sitting for the whole next year. I even had a brace for the shower.

As they slowly started bringing me off the morphine and my mind started coming back to earth, I started acting like my normal self again. They removed me from intensive care and put me on another floor. Even though the recovery process was long and painful, the doctors, nurses, and my family tried to make it as fun as possible.

Then came the day that I had long awaited — going home day, but, there was a set back. On the day we were getting ready to leave the hospital, some thieves broke into our van and my grandparents car and stole a lot of stuff. Although, we lost many personal belongings, God's hand of protection was still upon us. They took everything that was in a bag, except for the bag that contained all of my ventilator circuits that I would need when I got home.

Me being a tender 10-year-old and the shock of something like this happening to me, I cried and said, "I wish Jesus would come back right now so that judgment would fall upon them."

I look back on it now and God was trying to teach me a couple of lessons: one, that you have to forgive someone no matter what they do to you. Second of all, Jesus reminded me that just as the thieves came unexpectedly, He also is returning again as a thief in the night.

After the police were called and reports filled out, we left the hospital and made our six-hour trip back home where my Uncle Randy, Aunt Donna, MaRanda, and Natasha were waiting for me with welcome-home posters and balloons.

As that year progressed, strength returned back to my body and I was able to go back to school. I was thankful in more ways than one for my 5th grade graduation. Not only had I made it through elementary school, a day the doctor's never thought I would see, but the mountain that I had faced at the beginning of that school year, God had plucked up and cast into the sea.

I knew God had spared my life for His purpose.

13

Accepting the Call

A h, middle school, the land of learning and preteen stupidity all in one. Most of my friends were worrying about their first girlfriend and first pimple. I, on the other hand, was trying to figure out exactly where I "fit in" in life. I joined every kind of club that I could join. I was in:

- student council and Vice President in 8th grade
- Fellowship of Christian Athletes and President in 8th grade
- National Junior Honor Society
- wrote articles for the school paper
- part of the football and basketball teams during 7th and 8th grade

I seemed to "fit in" fairly well and through grade school and middle school had made some life long friendships which, if I tried to list each and everyone, I would be sure to leave one out and would never want to leave the impression that any one was more important than the other.

In the course of middle school, I also faced one of many challenges of being in a wheelchair that were to come in my life. It was during the student council field trip that for the first time in my life, I faced discrimination and realized not everyone saw me as an equal. The first part of the field trip was to a roller skating rink. It was a private party and the rink was only occupied by our students.

As always, I made the best of my situation, put on a pair of roller skates just to be able to feel the sensation of rolling my feet back and forth on my foot pedals and hit the rink in my wheelchair with my friends. After completing my first lap, the "old grumpy" owner came storming onto the skating floor and told me in a mean, hateful voice to get off the skating floor.

I was in complete shock and did not understand what had just taken place. I was trying to figure out what I had done wrong, which was nothing. I was just having fun with my friends the only way I could.

This is when my mother intervened. It was then that I comprehended the true protective instincts that God has instilled in mothers. The man tried to explain to my mom that he was concerned that I could injure someone in my wheelchair. He would have really freaked out if I had taken out the rope that I had brought along to pull my friends behind me. My mom tried to explain that the kids that were there had been around me for many years and they always watched out for me and I for them.

However, no amount of explanation would he hear. His mind was made up. I was not allowed on the skating floor. This upset my mom which in turn upset my grandpa. Let's just say, it is a good thing both are good Christian people. The teachers offered to take everyone and leave, but I did not want to be the cause for them to not have fun.

So, as I left in tears at a young, sensitive age of 12, I was crushed and heartbroken and felt as if I had faced the devil himself. My field trip that day that started out with friends wound up being a trip with my mom, grandpa, and nanny to Toys R Us and Vintage Stock where I got a Michael Jordan Starting Line Up. Although my mom understands that happiness cannot be bought, that day she would have given me the whole world if she could have.

Middle school years were definitely learning years for me, probably not so much the school curriculum that I learned about, but life lessons.

It was also during these years that the calling that God had placed in my life from the beginning to preach the gospel began to burn in my heart and as the prophet, Jeremiah, put it, "His word was in my heart as a burning fire shut up in my bones."

All I needed was an opportunity.

My English teacher my 6th grade year was Mrs. Dillon. She and her husband, Mr. Dillon, who I would later have as a teacher in High School, were youth ministers for an Assembly of God church in Vinita, Oklahoma, at that time. Mrs. Dillon, my mom, a friend of mine since first grade, Zack Wyatt, and I were visiting one day before class started. Mrs. Dillon was telling us about her daughter, Desiree, how she would be singing at the state Fine Arts Competition for the Assemblies of God.

I curiously asked, "What is the Fine Arts Festival?"

She explained that the Fine Arts Festival was an annual event where youth from the state of Oklahoma gather to showcase their talents for the Lord and if they were good enough would go on to the national Fine Arts Festival which was being held in Kansas City, Missouri, that particular year. She then began to list the different categories such as solo, sign language, drama, but I didn't hear any others after she said, "preaching."

The moment she said, "preaching," it caught my ear and attention. I immediately said in an excited voice, "I could preach!"

But, the funny thing is, I had never preached a sermon in my life. That didn't matter because the calling was there and the door was opened.

Without hesitation, Mrs. Dillon invited me to go with their church and said she would confirm it with their pastor to make sure it would be okay. Everything had been set in motion.

In March of 2001, I traveled to Oklahoma City for my first "official sermon." The morning of the competition, March 10, we got there early. Due to limited space at the church for all the different categories, the preaching competition was being held at the Oklahoma State University Extension Class Rooms. The wheelchair entrance was mid level with steps leading down or up. Therefore, I could not access the stage like everyone else, so they had to improvise for me.

I was so nervous as I watched the other, more experienced teens deliver their sermons. My heart was in my throat and my stomach was doing flip flops. I was praying two things, "Lord, send your fire and help me not to mess up."

Time for me seemed to almost stand still as the man announced at the microphone, "Next up, we have Jacob Berry."

So right from where I was sitting, I elevated my wheelchair. With my mom by my left side to be my interpreter because of my speech impediment, I prepared to deliver my very first sermon titled, "No Regrets."

I realized it was at that appointed time, at the age of 12 years old, I had accepted God's calling on my life to preach the gospel.

All I can recall as I began to deliver my short two-minute sermon was seeing the tears stream down the audiences' faces.

As the sermon came to a close, I knew it wasn't the end, but only the beginning as I received a Superior rating with invitation to the National Level of Fine Arts.

I knew exactly where I "fit in."

14

The
Anointing

The National Fine Arts Festival, Kansas City, Missouri, August 2001, appeared to this small, crippled, country boy as a massive extravaganza full of sights, sounds and lots of young people from all over the United States. As I watched in amazement at all the hustle and bustle of the throngs of people, I wondered to myself, "What am I doing here?" It did help and give us reassurance that we had once again made this trip with the Dillon family, who were a little more seasoned at this.

After I received my pulse back, we decided, we are here, might as well jump in and take part. So we went to registration and picked up our official badges and packet. We scanned the program to find the day, time and place for the

Short Sermon competition. I was to preach on Wednesday, August 8, 2001 at 8:56 AM in room 4300G. I was one of the youngest competitors of the 247 that were participating in the Short Sermon category. The average age in the Short Sermon category ranged from 16 to 18 years old. I was an inexperienced, intimidated 12 year old.

Other preaching competitions where I would preach, in the coming years, had age divisions, but not here. The 6th graders competed with the 12th graders. There was no turning back now.

Wednesday morning came and I only thought I was nervous when I had preached in Oklahoma City. That was nothing compared to what I was feeling this day. As in the words of my Grandpa Mercer, "I was as nervous as a cat at a dog show."

We arrived at the convention center early enough to watch and listen to the competitors that went before me. As I listened to the one that preached right before me, I can recall thinking to myself, "Wow, that one preaches like a REAL preacher and I have to follow that."

And follow it, I did. The announcer stepped to the microphone and again, I heard those words, "Up next is Jacob Berry."

Silence fell upon the crowd as I made my way to the front. As all eyes were on me, the job at hand was to turn their eyes upon Jesus. I once again delivered the same "No Regrets" sermon that I had delivered in Oklahoma City, never anticipating that I would advance to the Final Round of competition and be doing it again.

After I had finished with my competition, I felt a little more relaxed. Later that afternoon, after the judges had submitted their evaluations and scores, we went to the convention center lobby to watch the results being displayed on several big screen televisions. I can't tell you the joy and excitement that rushed through my soul as I watched my name scroll across the big screen with the words ADVANCED written beside it.

Forty six of the 247 that had been in the Short Sermon category had advanced to the final round and I was one of those 46. This meant I had the opportunity to preach yet again.

Thursday, August 9th, "Here we go again," I thought as I woke up that morning more nervous than the day before. We got to the same room at the convention center and there were lines waiting outside the doors to go in. The crowd had multiplied because this was the final round. I entered the room and anxiously awaited my turn.

I don't think I heard much of the sermons from the others before me as I fervently prayed. However, I did hear the one right before and wouldn't you know it, the same boy that preached before me in the first round that preached like he had been doing it for years was the same one that preached before me in the final round. I had to follow him again.

There was not an empty seat in the room and people were even standing lined up along the walls as it came my turn to preach. I began to preach the sermon just like the two previous times. I was about midway through preaching the sermon when suddenly I felt something that I had never felt before. I realized it was not what I felt, but who I felt. I felt the blessed, sweet Holy Ghost of Heaven fall upon me and consume my whole body, heart and soul with an unquenchable burning fire.

As I continued the sermon, I could feel His mighty anointing power. The fire had rested upon me and the anointing had run down me and onto my wheelchair as the precious ointment upon the head that ran down upon the beard, even Aaron's beard, that went down to the skirts of his garments as described in Psalm 133 verse 2. Some call it the anointing. Some call it being filled with the Holy Ghost. Others call it baptism by fire. At the age of 12, I wasn't sure what to call it, all I knew was that I FELT it and at that moment everything for me had changed.

My life would never be the same.

As the sermon came to a close, God's holy presence had not only filled my soul and my cup, but it had overflowed into the room.

When we made our way through the crowd to exit the room, I tried my best to get to my Grandpa because I knew with his wisdom he would understand what had just happened to me. As we made it outside the room into the lobby, I embraced my Grandpa and said, "Grandpa, I felt the Holy Ghost."

With tears in his eyes, Grandpa said, "I know you did. I can see the glory on your face."

Unbeknown to me, as my interpreter, my mom must have been feeling the same spirit that I was, because a pastor, Pastor Mark Wright, from Mooresville, Indiana, approached her and asked, "Does he travel?"

My mom, in shock with the question, replied, "That is Jacob's desire to travel and preach the gospel."

Pastor Mark proceeded to tell my mom that he would like for me to come to his church in Indiana. After they exchanged contact information to make the arrangements, my mom asked herself, "What just happened and what is going to happen?"

At that moment, however, she knew whatever it was, God was in complete control and He knew exactly what He was doing with my life.

Several months later, during my 7th grade year, we received a call from Pastor Mark and a date was set in February 2002 for me to preach during the Sunday services at Springhill Christian Center in Mooresville, Indiana. On a cold, cloudy day, my family, including my grandpa and nanny and my grandma, made my very first evangelistic trip. I only had one sermon and my testimony, but that is all I needed for that particular day. The Lord always provides what we need when we need it.

It would be four and a half years later in September of 2006, at the age of 16 that I would return to Springhill Christian

Center in Mooresville, Indiana, to preach my very first revival.

I will always be grateful to Pastor Mark Wright and the faith and obedience to God that he had when he gave the opportunity to an inexperienced, young preacher boy, in his journey to become a man of God to preach the gospel to his large congregation at Springhill Christian Center.

However, with that said, none of this would have ever been possible had it not been for a 6th grade teacher believing in one of her students.

15

Growing in Wisdom and in Truth

Theoretically speaking, a plant cannot grow without rain and with rain comes storms. Silver cannot be refined without going through the fire. A sports team cannot become champions without facing adversity. Sometimes, growing up means growing out of some things. This was the case for me as I entered my freshman year of High School.

The only reason that I always looked forward to school starting wasn't for the academics, but rather that it meant that football season was also starting. For two years, during my seventh and eighth grade years, I was permitted to be on the football field with our school's football team. However, as my freshman year began, I was informed that I could no longer participate with the football team in that way. Our school system utilized our local Junior College Stadium for football games and I was no longer allowed on the football field during games even though it was the same field that I had been on the two previous years. The following is an excerpt from the letter we received from our school system stating their reasons that I was not allowed to be a part of the team:

> "It is with regret that we cannot honor your request for Jacob to be considered as an honorary member of the 9th grade football team and participate as such during scheduled football games. After much discussion with NEO A & M College officials, the final determination was that all individuals confined to a wheelchair are denied access to the field or track area while games are in session. We are in agreement that for the safety of all involved, viewing of the game must be done from the designated handicapped area."

I was "denied access" to the field because I was in a wheelchair. Now, I not only faced my own physical limitations of not being able to participate in a game I loved, but man and regulations were placing limitations on me also. My mom did all she could to fight for my rights, but they would not change the regulation.

The college, however, had to make some major renovations to their stadium to make it more handicapped accessible.

Even though it didn't work out the way I thought it should, the stadium was now more accessible for others in wheelchairs wanting to attend a football game. You see, sometimes our thoughts are not God's thoughts and our ways are not His ways.

"For my thoughts are not your thoughts, neither are your ways my ways, saith the LORD.

For as the heavens are higher than the earth, so are my ways higher than your ways, and my thoughts than your thoughts."
— Isaiah 55:8-9 (KJV)

Later my freshman year, after the football season had ended, my school hired a new head football coach and I happened to have him as a teacher for Oklahoma History. As each class began, he would play a little trivia game with the class. The questions ranged anywhere from sports to politics. One day, he asked the question, "Who won the first Super Bowl and who was the starting quarterback?"

Some of the answers flew out from students that happened to be a part of the school's football team, but none of them knew the correct answer. With excitement, I raised my hand and confidently answered, "The Green Bay Packers won the first Super Bowl and Bart Starr was the winning quarterback."

The coach was impressed. He and I hit it off from there. One day after class, he told my mom that he would like for me to come out and be a part of his football team, stating that I had more passion and probably as much knowledge for the game as any player he had.

My mom explained what had transpired at the beginning of the year, how they wouldn't let me on the field. He replied, "I don't understand it; however, I know I can't go against the regulation, but anybody could see what an inspiration that he could be to a team."

My mom thought about this for about a week. She then approached the coach with an idea. Since it was a public school, she wasn't for sure, but asked him if he allowed the football boys to say prayer before a game. He said he allowed them to recite the Lord's Prayer. She then told him that it would mean more to me than being on the field to come in the locker room before each home game and lead the boys in this prayer.

He agreed to this idea and for the three remaining years that I was in High School, I went in the locker room and led the football boys in the Lord's Prayer before each home game. Before the last home football game of my senior year, I went into the locker room with my grandpa like I normally did. I asked the coach if I could say something. He permitted it and I told the boys, "It has been a privilege and an honor to pray with you these past three years. I want you to know if you need anything, all you have to do is pray to Jesus. And if you don't know how to pray, just pray the same prayer that we have been praying before each home game." As silence fell in the locker room, we began the Lord's Prayer.

What I couldn't see at the beginning of my freshman year, God knew my desire to be a part of the football team I would out grow. However, my desire to be on the football field did not diminish, but rather transformed into something greater.

One day, sitting in Biology class, I was daydreaming as usual. My mom tapped me on the shoulder and told me that I needed to listen because they were reviewing for a test the next day. I am not sure how she always knew when I wasn't paying attention. Anyway, she knew she hadn't snapped me out of my daydream, so she asked me, "What are you thinking about?"

I said, "Well, I decided since I will never play football in a stadium, maybe one day I will preach in one." Needless to say, mom let me slide that day and we studied that night for the test.

Football and preaching wasn't the only thing on my mind during my high school years. As any other typical male teenager, I liked girls. Through my experiences and observations, I came to the conclusion and told my mom one day at school, "Chicks just dig guys that can walk."

My mom told me that if God wanted me to have a girl in my life, she would like me for who I was and wouldn't see my disability. I did meet a special girl, Christina, at church camp and she did see past my wheelchair. Even though she lived an hour away, we "dated" for about a year and a half. Ironically, we met at church camp and, unexpected to me, broke up at church camp. I was heart broken, but I recovered as all young people do.

Now, I had no distractions and my mind could be totally focused on my calling in life, to preach the gospel. I remember growing up watching on television, a distinguished white headed preacher, the great evangelist, Dr. Billy Graham. While viewing his telecast, I noticed the simplicity of the gospel message. The messages that he preached were clear and to the point.

I was privileged to attend one of his last crusades in 2005 at the Ford Center in Oklahoma City, Oklahoma. I was amazed that in the midst of this mammoth venue and vast audience that you could sense the mighty presence of the Lord upon Dr. Billy Graham as he entered the arena and took the platform. That night he preached a message from John Chapter 14 verse 6: "I am the way, the truth, and the life."

As in most of the messages that I have heard him preach, he reminded the people and told them that, "God loves you." His ministry intrigued me and impacted my life at a young age — so much so that I did my Senior research paper on Dr. Billy Graham. After my research, now, more than ever, I prayed that I would have the same integrity and same impact on the world as this great man of God.

Years later, as I was evangelizing in North Carolina, a pastor's wife who worked for Samaritan's Purse, a ministry of Dr. Billy Graham's son, Franklin Graham, made arrangements for me to tour Samaritan's Purse and meet Mr. Sam McGinn. It was during another trip to Samaritan's Purse, while having lunch with Mr. McGinn, that I shared my respect and admiration that I had for Dr. Billy Graham and how I would love to meet him.

At this point in his life, however, his health, but not his mind, was failing and he did not meet with many people. Even after he shared that information with me, Mr. McGinn told me to write a letter to Dr. Graham and he would do what he could to make sure that he received it. So I shared my heart and the following is a copy of the letter that I sent:

September 17, 2010

Dear Dr. Billy Graham:

Your ministry has had a profound influence on my life. Ever since I was a little child, even though I had great physical challenges, I can remember saying, "I am going to grow up and be a great preacher like Billy Graham." I am now 21 years old and my physical challenges of being in a wheelchair and ventilator dependent since 11 days old has not diverted my soul's desire to preach the gospel around the world and to see multitudes come to the saving knowledge of Jesus Christ.

When I was reading the Bible in II Kings Chapter 2 about Elijah and Elisha, I thought to myself what a great gift it would be if the Lord would allow me to meet His servant, Billy Graham. I would consider it such an honor just to be in the presence of such a mighty man of God, and even a greater honor if this great man of God could pray for me and my ministry. I would be as Elisha to Elijah and ask, "that a double portion of thy spirit be upon me." I know the power does not come from you, but from the power that lives within you.

I realize that your health is declining and my dreams of meeting you will only be if it is the will of our Heavenly Father. I fully understand the day to day struggles when your health is compromised as I struggle each day with muscular dystrophy and being on a ventilator.

Thank you for taking the time to listen to the desires of my heart. I pray that someday, I can be used by our Heavenly Father to be an encouragement to you and to make an impact on the world for Jesus just as you and The Billy Graham Evangelistic Association.

Humbly Living the Gift,
Jacob Berry, Jacob Berry Ministries, Inc.

Six months later, I received a letter from Dr. Graham's personal secretary stating how my letter had been shared with Dr. Graham and as he was told about my desire for his prayers that he bowed his head in prayer for me and my ministry. What a blessing to know that someone is praying for you.

I would need all the prayers that I could get as I only thought I had faced adversity my freshman year with the football issue. That was nothing compared to what lay ahead during my sophomore year as I endured one of the most difficult trials in my life.

In March of 2005, during spring break, I was struck with a severe illness called Clostridium Difficile, C-Difficile for short. At first we thought it was just the run of the mill, typical stomach virus. But as the days progressed, I kept getting worse. The doctors didn't know what was causing the problem. All the blood work and other tests for C-Difficile kept coming up negative.

The tests may have been negative, but I was positive I had something and it was eating my life away. Through the frustration, dehydration, and months of reoccurring hospitalizations that lasted through spring and summer, for the first time in my life, I simply lost the will to live.

One night, lying in the hospital after I had lost 20 pounds and only weighing 92 pounds to begin with, I began to cry and said, "I'm tired, just take me off the ventilator, I want to go home."

My family knew I wasn't talking about leaving the hospital and going home, but rather I was talking about leaving this painful world and going to my home in Heaven. My mom had held together fairly well through all this, but this is when she lost it. She began crying and leaned over in the bed and took me in her arms as best she could and hugged me and said, "You can't go!"

My dad couldn't take it either. He got on the phone with Pastor Mark Wright from Indiana and asked him to pray. Pastor Mark asked to speak to me. Over the phone he prayed for me and encouraged me, saying, "Your job is not done yet. God still has work for you. You are coming to Indiana in July to preach at our Faith and Freedom Festival."

As he prayed for me, I'll be honest, I really didn't feel any better. Later that night at about two o'clock in the morning, I was awake because of my sickness, and the Lord gave me a wondrous thought, "One day our true Independence Day is coming and we will be free from all burdens, sickness, disease, sorrow, pain, and all of our tears will be wiped away."

That thought alone, gave me the strength and determination to fight and overcome this trial no matter how long or how hot the trial was. Through all the many tests that were done, an old fashion doctor that happened to be working in the ER when I had another relapse told us that even though the tests showed negative for the C-Diff, I had the classic symptoms. He suggested an old remedy that he had used on another patient that could not be cured of this illness, and sure enough after five months of fighting this illness, that doctor was right. As I look back on all of this, I believe God was preparing me for something special.

Although I was still fighting C-Difficile, that summer we went to the Free Will Baptist Nationals in Louisville, Kentucky. I was entered in the 10-minute short sermon competition. It was comparable to the Fine Arts Festival that I had preached at in Kansas City, Missouri. I was the last competitor in that category that day. My sermon title was "Jesus Is My Best Friend."

As I began to preach, that same Holy Ghost from Heaven that fell in Kansas City in 2001 fell again in Louisville, Kentucky, in 2005. God had complete control of me and my wheelchair. I took off preaching down the center of the aisle and could care less about the ten minute time limit, all I wanted to do was obey God.

Thirty minutes later, as I closed the sermon, we felt like we had been in an old fashion camp meeting. I am not quite sure if there had ever been shouting and praising the Lord during the short sermon competition like we experienced that day. I knew that I had lost the competition because I had gone over the time limit, but those who obey God will always be winners.

There happened to be several preachers from the state of Tennessee and one from North Carolina in the room while I was preaching and after I was finished, they approached me and asked the same question, "Does he travel?"

Again, my mom answered, "That is his desire to travel and preach the gospel."

My last two years of High School would be spent doing just that, traveling and preaching the gospel.

After my trial with C-Difficile, my mom realized that sitting in a classroom everyday and taking every test that everyone else took was no longer important. I had proven myself that I could do it. It was time to move on with my life. I had been on an Individualized Educational Plan (IEP) because of my disability during my school years, but never really "individualized" my education that much. Since my mom had gone to school with me all my life, it was determined by the IEP team that during my Junior and Senior year my school work could be done at home and modified to my needs. So, I began to travel greater distances and preach more often.

I had received my License to preach February 9, 2005. Six months later, in August of 2005, I went before the ordaining board. One of the delegates asked, "What would you do if we don't ordain you?"

My answer was simple and to the point, "I will preach anyway, because I know God has called me."

The ordaining board approved me for ordination and on October 15, 2005, at the age of 16, two days before turning 17, I was ordained in a service led by Evangelist Danny Ledbetter as a minister of the gospel of Jesus Christ. The ordination service was not only an ordination service, but also a celebration service as family, friends and ministers gathered to celebrate all the miracles that God had performed in my life to prepare me for His service.

As I received my charge, I perceived the seriousness of the responsibility that came with the calling on my life. I also felt a sense of humility and wondered, "Who Am I to partake in Thy Service, Oh, Lord, for I am as Moses, slow of speech?" But the Lord answered me with the same thing that he told Moses.

> "And the LORD said unto him, Who hath made man's mouth? or who maketh the dumb, or deaf, or the seeing, or the blind? have not I the LORD? Now therefore go, and I will be with thy mouth, and teach thee what thou shalt say."
> — Exodus 4:11-12 (KJV)

16

Evangelism and Graduation

During the early days of this ministry, besides our trip to Mooresville, Indiana, we were traveling to different local places sharing my testimony, but as I grew in the Lord, so, too, did the ministry. After my ordination, I was now not only preaching single services, but holding evangelistic revivals and traveling great distances.

In the beginning, my dad would use his vacation time for the evangelistic trips. We would load the back of our Ford Van to the ceiling with all of my medical equipment, medical supplies, food, and regular suitcases.

On one of these trips we were traveling to Vilonia, Arkansas. It was a beautiful Saturday morning. I was to preach the next Sunday morning in Vilonia and that Sunday night in Van Buren. I was studying and praying as we traveled down the highway. My dad was at the wheel and my mom was sleeping, as usual. It was about eleven o'clock in the morning and we had just passed the golf course in Bella Vista, Arkansas.

All of a sudden this big buck deer came out of no where, took one jump and then another right into our van. I could see his big rack coming straight for me. Was I scared? Of course, I was scared, too scared to even holler. Out of instinct, I just turned my head to shield my eyes from the flying glass and braced myself for the impact. Miraculously, before the deer's head hit me, something caused the deer's back side to jerk around and bust out the back window causing his head to jerk away from me. Of course we know that "something" was God's Hand. My mom woke up to the CRASH of the windows shattering. She flipped out when she saw me. I was covered in glass, but only my thumb was cut, a tiny cut at that.

After the Bella Vista sheriff's department came, we went to the Bentonville hospital emergency room to have me checked out for any unseen injuries. After using sophisti-cated medical equipment, a vacuum cleaner to clean me and my wheelchair up, the only injury I had was my tiny cut on my thumb. I felt much better after I got cleaned up.

During this time, my Grandpa and Nanny were going to come up and help us get the glass out of the van so we could get it home. We thought the services were going to have to be canceled, because I can't go anywhere without my wheel-chair, it carries my life support and there was no way to transport my wheelchair without my van. I believe God used my Uncle Randy. Instead of my Nanny coming with my Grandpa and driving their car, my Uncle Randy came with my Grandpa and drove his Yukon.

God gave my mom the idea that maybe we could rent a U-Haul to transport my wheelchair and drive my Uncle Randy's Yukon so we could continue the trip and do God's work. My Uncle Randy and my Grandpa really wanted me to come home. We made a few phone calls and were able to get a U-Haul. After stopping at Lowe's to get plywood for a ramp, we were back on the road to Vilonia Arkansas. I was in the Yukon and my wheelchair was in the U-Haul. Uncle Randy and Grandpa drove our van back home to Miami.

We finally made our destination that night at about 9:00 pm. The next morning I preached in Vilonia. God moved and nine people rededicated their lives to Christ. We made Van Buren and I preached the evening service. God moved and, again, one man was saved.

Because ten people's lives were changed by the power of God, anything I encountered that Saturday was worth it all.

Renting the U-Haul gave us the idea that it would make traveling in the van a little easier if we pulled a trailer to haul all of our stuff. So, for the next two years we traveled from coast to coast in our Ford Van pulling our little red trailer. We went from California to North Carolina and witnessed many miracles and many make commitments to Christ and lives that were forever changed.

Also, on our journeys, we have had the rare privilege to meet many Southern Gospel Greats on the east coast and on the west coast, movie and television stars.

God never ceased to amaze me as He worked His wonders in all different ways. During a meeting in Tennessee, there was a young boy that suffered with autism. It was difficult for him to stay calm and remain in a church service and he would never allow anyone to touch him. But this night was different.

After service, with the spirit of God still hovering in the air, with tears in his eyes, his father brought him forward and asked if I would pray for him. I stretched forth my hand to his and without hesitation he held my hand and stayed calm

Jacob & Mom at TBN studios meeting Mr. T
and Matt Crouch

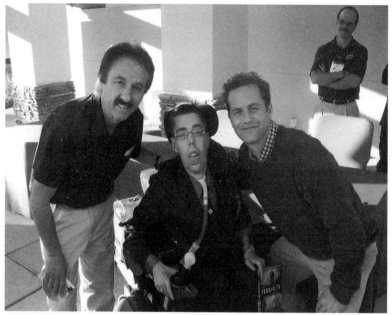

Jacob with Ray Comfort and Kirk Cameron

as other men of God gathered round about him and laid their hands on him to pray. A year later, when I returned to this area for another meeting, this same young boy that struggled to sit through a church service, stood in church before the congregation and sang a solo special.

There would be more miracles ahead. I was only 16 when we traveled to North Carolina. Six churches laid aside their differences and came together for a community-wide revival. It was a meeting that had been covered with prayers and many hours of preparation and visitation before we even arrived. When God's people come together and dwell in unity, in one mind and one accord, expect great things to happen. There was report that 48 people had made commitments to the Lord in that one week of revival. We have made many trips back to that area for services and what a blessing to see some of those that made commitments during our first trip stay true to the faith.

It was during one of these return trips to North Carolina that we met a special little fellow named Briar who was born with the same type of muscular dystrophy that I have. When we were first introduced, my heart was captured as this little boy, lying in his bed, moved his little right hand, the only muscle function that he is capable of, and held my hand.

One rare day when I was feeling a little sorry for myself because of my speech impediment and squeaky voice, the Lord brought my mind to little Briar who was born with no vocal chords and I thought, "Who am I to complain? The

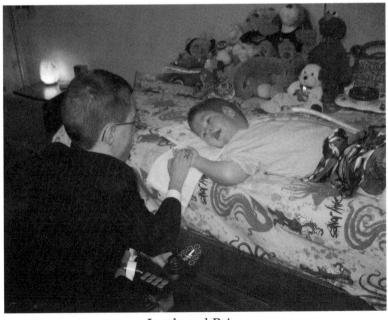

Jacob and Briar

Lord gave me a voice and I am going to use it to glorify Him."

Even though Briar may not be able to vocalize, the Lord still uses him to bring joy to his family and to anyone who meets him as his smile can light up any room. May that be said of us, for sometimes the power is not necessarily in the words we say, but how we live and the joy of the Lord that we radiate to others.

We have met many people, made countless friends, and etched in our mind special memories that will never be forgotten. It was through some of these acquaintances that I heard about The Super Bowl of Camp Meetings held every second week in January at the First Free Will Baptist Church in Seffner, Florida, and I was told that I needed to attend no matter what it took.

After much prayer and consulting with other ministries, we felt it was the Lord's will and made preparations to attend. There was a slight bump in the road, two weeks before we were scheduled to leave; I unexpectedly had to go through a painful emergency surgery. We were uncertain if I would be able to travel all the way from Oklahoma to Florida, because the healing process was to take six weeks. I was bound and determined to go anyway and got clearance from the doctor. We stopped at another church to preach in the Florida panhandle before driving on south to Seffner.

We arrived at the camp meeting on Monday night. When we pulled in the crowded parking lot of this big church and people were everywhere, being from a small town and small church, my mom turned to my dad and asked, "What are we doing here?"

My dad being the more experienced traveler, due to his job, reassured my mom that God was in control. It also helped when we ran into the minister who had done my ordination service and his family. We also had made plans to meet another pastor we had met in Arkansas. The Seffner church was his home church that he had grown up in. I remember thinking, "This is going to be awesome." And awesome it was, right from the first note of music.

Through the chain reaction of events that had happened and different people I had met, doors opened. The pastor of this church, Reverend Roger Duncan, who had never met me but had heard about me, called Reverend Keith Hatton, the pastor from Arkansas, up to the stage and asked if I was the young man he had been hearing about. Brother Keith said, "Yes, this is him."

Brother Roger Duncan said, "I want him to testify."

If you think my mom was nervous when she pulled in the parking lot, you should have seen her then, because if I had to testify in front of 1100 people that meant mom had to interpret in front of 1100 people.

After the congregational singing, I was called to the front of the church to give my testimony. Brother Keith introduced me with the scripture:

> "But God hath chosen the foolish things of the world to confound the wise; and God hath

chosen the weak things of the world to confound the things which are mighty;

And base things of the world, and things which are despised, hath God chosen, yea, and things which are not, to bring to nought things that are:

That no flesh should glory in his presence."
— 1 Corinthians 1:27-29 (KJV)

With that said, I proceeded to share my testimony of the great things that God has done in my life, how He has helped me, through His blood, to overcome muscular dystrophy and live a victorious life. Shouts of praise and tears of joy filled the sanctuary as the Holy Ghost stirred the hearts from the oldest to the youngest.

Following my testimony, Reverend Brian Baer, from Lucasville, Ohio, preached a timely message that could have only been orchestrated by God called "Is It Worth It?" I can answer that question by saying, sitting in this wheel-chair everyday, suffering through the many surgeries and being dependent on others for my needs, Praise God, it is still worth it all!

After a lively, high octane, Holy Ghost filled service, I was approached by the director of Evangelistic Outreach of Ironton, Ohio, Dr. Calvin Ray Evans, a highly respected prominent preacher of this day and age. He asked for our permission to use the video of my testimony from that evening on the television program of Evangelistic Outreach. Without hesitation, I gladly said, "Yes!"

The next night, from the pulpit, Dr. Evans announced that I would be preaching one night, alongside him and his assistant, Reverend Brian Baer at the Spring Jubilee, an evangelistic outreach event held every year the week following Mother's Day, in Lucasville, Ohio.

It has been proven that many anointed ministries have never been the same after attending the Seffner Camp Meeting. I can say for a fact that this meeting had an impact on Jacob Berry Ministries being a full-time ministry, as requests for me to preach began to grow. My mom knew this meant more time on the road and more time that my dad would be away from his job. She recalls one night in the motel praying, "Lord, we can't do this. Joe needs his job, because Jacob needs health insurance."

The Lord's answer to her was as clear as if He were sitting across the room speaking to her as He said, "Jacob is here on this earth for one purpose; to preach the gospel and if he is not able to do that, he might as well be home with me."

Needless to say, my mom decided she wanted to keep me around a little longer and we found ourselves traveling in our van with our little red trailer to Lucasville, Ohio, in May of 2007, one week before I graduated from High School, for Spring Jubilee.

I was full of excitement and anticipation during the trip to Ohio. Spring Jubilee was a popular event for the tri-state area of Ohio, Kentucky, and West Virginia. It was held at the Scioto County Fair Grounds in an open air covered building that was converted for this one week into a church.

I wasn't quite sure what to expect, but I was coming expecting. Up until this time, I had never been in services with any of the great Southern Gospel singing groups that were scheduled each night of Spring Jubilee. Monday night's singing group was a crowd favorite, The McKameys.

Right before they came to sing, I shared my testimony. My mom only thought she was nervous in Florida in front of 1100 people. This night there were over 2000 people. I couldn't believe that I was on the same stage with the world famous McKameys watching live Peg McKamey get happy and kick her shoes off and wave her white hanky as she sang, "God On The Mountain." After the excitement of Monday night came nervousness, as I was scheduled to preach Tuesday night.

Jacob & Southern Gospel Greats — The McKamey's

I was not the only one nervous; even my dad was nervous and he didn't even have to speak in front of anybody. That night, sensing my nervousness, before the meeting, Calvin Ray gave me some sound advice, "Don't be overwhelmed, just preach the word under the anointing."

Mike Blanton & Evidence was one of the groups singing that night, along with The Spencers. Dr. Calvin Ray Evans brought me over and presented me with a graduation gift from the church he pastored, Rubyville Community Church. Every graduate of Rubyville Community Church receives a Bible for graduation and I was blessed that they had honored me in that way. Calvin Ray then shared with the 1300 people that had gathered that evening for service about my difficulties traveling in a van with a trailer. He then pointed and told me to look to my left and as I turned, there sat a Motor Home. As he handed the keys to me, I put them in my pocket. Our prayers had been answered. We had been praying for several months for a motor home and had just sent out a ministry newsletter, which Calvin Ray Evans and Evangelistic Outreach had no knowledge of, 13 days before asking others to help us pray for this need in our ministry.

After the exhilaration of receiving this miracle, God still had more in store as His message was still to be delivered. That night, I preached a sermon titled, "Living on the Fingertips of God." The message was derived from the fiery sermon, "Sinners in the Hands of an Angry God" preached by Reverend Jonathan Edwards July 8, 1741. When it was all said and done, there were 13 people that took the hand of God and discovered the love and protection of living in the center of His mighty outstretched hand.

Our souls were so filled up that I wanted to stay all week, but my High School graduation was that weekend. I did get to stay for Jubilee one more night. That night before the Spencer family took the stage, I was asked to do a song in sign language which began a move of people to the altar giving thanks for their many blessings.

Not only that night, but everyday, I am so thankful for the many blessings in my life. I have been blessed to return every year since to Spring Jubilee and preach on Tuesday night. I was also blessed to preach at Day Star Studios in Ashland, Kentucky for a special night of remembrance at the Calvin and Doris Evans Memorial Camp Meeting, a meeting that honors the parents of Dr. Calvin Ray Evans and founders of Evangelistic Outreach. Evangelistic Outreach has been a help to the growth of our ministry. They have given us support, guidance, and been a Godly example of what a ministry should be.

During that one week in May of 2007, one chapter in my life was opened at Spring Jubilee and another closed that weekend during my High School graduation. As the other students celebrated their accomplishment of finishing high school, this day to me was not only a celebration of this achievement, but the miracle that this day had come in my life.

The highlight of the ceremony for me was when I was allowed to give the invocation and proudly give thanks in the name above all names, Jesus Christ, the one who had given me life and the opportunity to celebrate this graduation day. I was grateful for all my family and friends who were with me on that day to help me commemorate this momentous occasion. I graduated on a Saturday and left on Monday to continue with the chapter that had been opened at Spring Jubilee.

That chapter wasn't the only thing that opened up. At the Carolina Mountain Youth Retreat in Hayesville, North Carolina, the following weekend, Heaven got opened up. Never in my life have I experienced a move of God like that night.

The retreat was held outside under a tent with the beautiful Blue Ridge Mountains serving as the back drop. The setting was set for a perfect evening in the Lord. With the majority of the congregation being teenagers and young adults, the message the Lord had given me for that night was "Jesus Is My Best Friend." Countless teenagers, and even their

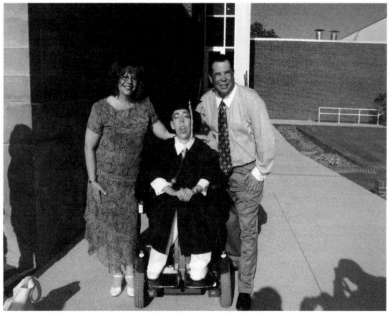

Jacob's High School graduation with Mom & Dad

parents, found that Best Friend that night that sticketh closer than a brother and committed their lives to their new found friend, Jesus Christ.

As the presence of the Lord lingered under the tent, so, too, did the altar service. The Lord moved upon Reverend Chris Rumfelt, the host pastor of this meeting, in such a mighty way that he quit singing, leaped from the stage with hands in the air and took off running into the field outside. As he was on his face before the Lord, the crowd and the praise migrated outside to him.

As the cries and the prayers were lifted toward Heaven, Heaven opened up. It was a clear night sky with no moon, only one single star could be seen and that star was shining brightly upon Brother Chris and the others as they sought the face of God.

Three hours later, after the service had ended, we looked to the sky and the star that had been shining upon us was gone. That night I knew that Heaven had opened up and God had smiled upon His children.

God has opened many doors and I have been given the opportunity to preach and share my testimony in all different venues: schools, colleges, and churches, ranging from a Christian Rock Concert to Old Fashioned Southern Gospel Tent Meetings. I have been in English speaking churches and Russian and Romanian speaking churches. Each meeting has been unique in its own way, but never compromising the message of the cross.

I am always willing to preach the gospel anywhere and everywhere, because Jesus said in Mark Chapter 16 verse 15:

> *"And he said unto them, Go ye into all the world, and preach the gospel to every creature."*
> — Mark 16:15 (KJV)

Therefore, under the anointing of the Holy Spirit, I have tried my best to passionately proclaim the gospel to a lost and dying world.

17

Stepping Into Adulthood

The words, "He could die prematurely, and if he does live, he will never amount to anything but be a vegetable all of his life," were words once used to describe me. But my family never believed these words and removed them from their vocabulary.

I am not a mistake, but the potter that created this little broken vessel knew His plans for me.

> "Before I formed thee in the belly I knew thee; and before thou camest forth out of the womb I sanctified thee, and I ordained thee a prophet unto the nations."
> — Jeremiah 1:5 (KJV)

Everyday, the potter gently takes me into His hands and continues to work on me and shape me.

On October 17, 2009, by God's grace, I had defeated all the laws of my disease, rising above all the doctor's expectations. My family gathered to rejoice what many thought would never happen as I turned 21 and stepped into adulthood.

I didn't really know what being an adult truly meant until the next summer. My Grandma Berry had gotten very sick and was near death. I was on my way home from a dentist appointment in Tulsa, Oklahoma when my cousin Glenna, who was helping my grandma, called and said that grandma needed to talk to me.

L to R: Mom, Dad and Grandma Berry and Jacob (center)
at Grandma's church.

128

I will never forget grandma's words when she simply said, "Jacob, I need you to release me."

I told her I already had a couple of weeks ago during the Carolina Mountain Youth Retreat during the singing. They were singing about Heaven and I got to thinking about my sick little grandma back home who so longed to go to that beautiful land where there is no sickness or pain. As they continued to sing, the tears began to flow as I realized how selfish I was being by wanting to keep her in this wicked, sinful world.

On June 16, 2010, Heaven gained another prayer warrior as my Grandma Berry went on to be with her Lord and Savior, the One whom she adored and loved.

Before her crossing, grandma called me to her bedside. As I sat in my wheelchair and held her frail and withered hand, she looked me in the eyes and with a weak, but stern voice, she said, "Jacob, promise me one thing. No matter what, keep preaching the gospel."

Trying to contain myself and keep a brave face, for I knew it wouldn't be long before the angels came to carry her home, I made her that promise. I also knew that I had truly stepped into adulthood.

Grandma's passing made me more aware that this world is vanity and our life is nothing more than a vapor in the wind, which today is and tomorrow is gone.

We were put on this earth for one purpose and that is to serve our Lord Jesus Christ every single day of our lives. My grandma left her heirs that legacy.

I made her that promise and I have every intention of keeping that promise.

18

Ministry Visions

Ever since I can remember, the Lord birthed in my spirit a vision to preach the gospel around the world. This vision, I am happy to report, is beginning to become a reality. In May 2006, Jacob Berry Ministries became a nonprofit 501(c)(3) corporation. Jacob Berry Ministries, Inc. is an inter-denominational ministry dedicated to preaching the gospel of Jesus Christ and seeing souls saved for His Kingdom.

During a board meeting to discuss new avenues for the ministry to reach more people for Christ, the statement was made that because I had lived past the doctor's expectations that I was a true miracle and I was living on a gift. Henceforth, the ministry's theme: Living the Gift.

Our logo reflects that:

Miracle On A Mission
JACOB BERRY
MINISTRIES™

Living the Gift™

Today, Jacob Berry Ministries has had the privilege to preach the gospel across the United States and through the aid of internet and DVD media in many parts of the world. We have seen the hand of God work many miracles in people's lives as countless lives have been touched and changed, bodies have been healed, people have been delivered from addictions, but best of all, souls have been saved.

Recently, we received report of a preacher in the Philippines who suffered physical challenges and could not walk. Someone would carry him on their back into the church house so he could share the message of the gospel and the love of Jesus Christ.

When I learned how this man would let nothing stop him from preaching, it tugged at my heart, knowing the struggles I personally have and I have the blessing of a power wheelchair. Through the help of the Lord and some generous people, Jacob Berry Ministries was able to donate a power chair to this preacher in the Philippines, giving him mobility and independence to preach the gospel.

Jacob preaching in 2011

I not only have the vision of Jacob Berry Ministries preaching the gospel but also of being an outreach and extension of God's love to the broken and battered vessels of the world.

Living the Gift

19

The
Dream

O ne night while sleeping, I had a dream. In this dream, I saw myself sitting in my wheelchair in the center of a plush green field with a blue sky above. Fencing the field were tall trees, as tall as redwoods.

As a gazed across the field, I saw a flock of sheep and there in the midst of the sheep stood the shepherd. The shepherd turned his head and saw me. He began to make his way through the sheep and walked toward me.

I could not see his face because the glory was too great, but I knew who He was when He reached out His hand to take my hand, and I saw the nail prints. I heard the sweetest, most loving, yet authoritative, voice say to me, "Jacob, I say unto you, ARISE!"

Immediately, with His help, I arose from my wheelchair and stood to me feet. I saw myself take my very first steps as I began to walk side by side, hand in hand with Jesus. I glanced back and saw my wheelchair burst into flames.

Then, I awoke and it was all a dream.

I rejoice in this fact, one day, when my eyes behold Him, my dream will become reality. I am going to walk down the streets of gold holding the hand of my best friend, my shepherd, Jesus Christ.

It is not simply that I am in a wheelchair that this dream will become reality. It is because Jesus Christ shed His blood and died on the cross for my healing and for my forgiveness of sins. He then rose triumphantly over the grave giving us hope of redemption and eternal life. Jesus did His part.

> *"But God commendeth his love toward us, in that, while we were yet sinners, Christ died for us."*
>
> — Romans 5:8 (KJV)

Now, we must do our part and realize that we are all sinners in need of a Savior.

> *"As it is written, There is none righteous, no, not one:"*
>
> — Romans 3:10 (KJV)

"For all have sinned, and come short of the glory of God;"
— Romans 3:23 (KJV)

"For the wages of sin is death; but the gift of God is eternal life through Jesus Christ our Lord."
— Romans 6:23 (KJV)

We all need to ask forgiveness and repent of our sins.

"That if thou shalt confess with thy mouth the Lord Jesus, and shalt believe in thine heart that God hath raised him from the dead, thou shalt be saved. For with the heart man believeth unto righteousness; and with the mouth confession is made unto salvation."
— Romans 10:9-10 (KJV)

"For whosoever shall call upon the name of the Lord shall be saved."
— Romans 10:13 (KJV)

"If we confess our sins, he is faithful and just to forgive us our sins, and to cleanse us from all unrighteousness."
— 1 John 1:9 (KJV)

After we have come to the cross and have confessed our sins, repented of our sins and have accepted the ultimate gift, Jesus Christ, as the Lord of our life, we then can begin "Living the Gift," living each day as Christ, for Christ, through the gift of salvation found only in Jesus Christ.

20

Living the Gift

Just because I am disabled does not mean that I am the only one that is living on a gift, because everyday that you live is a gift from God. Life is a gift and we should never take for granted what God has blessed us with.

There are many things that I cannot do that most people never consider as gifts from God. However, I have no regrets being me because I have Jesus in my heart and that is all I need and that is all anybody needs, because His grace is sufficient.

> *"And he said unto me, My grace is sufficient for thee: for my strength is made perfect in weakness. Most gladly therefore will I rather glory in*

my infirmities, that the power of Christ may rest upon me. Therefore I take pleasure in infirmities, in reproaches, in necessities, in persecutions, in distresses for Christ's sake: for when I am weak, then am I strong."
— 2 Corinthians 12:9-10 (KJV)

Everyday, I am "Living the Gift."

I may not be able to walk, but that will not stop me from walking with Jesus.

I may have a speech impediment, but that will not stop me from telling others about Jesus. I do have a voice and even if it doesn't sound like others, I am going to use my voice to boldly preach the gospel of Jesus Christ.

I can't eat, but that will not stop me from feasting on the manna from Heaven above.

I struggle with each breath I take, but that will not stop me from praising the Lord.

My life has been filled with ups and downs, twists and turns, trials and tribulations, but through it all, God has been there reminding me that I am not a mistake, but a gift from God and am able to do all things through Christ which strengthens me.

"I can do all things through Christ which strengtheneth me."
— Philippians 4:13 (KJV)

Current family picture

As the words of the song writer so eloquently put, "God has been my Father, my Savior, and my Friend. His love was my beginning and His love will be my end. I could spend forever trying to tell you everything He is, but the best way that I can say it, is this, God has been good in my life."

I still say, "I have been blessed with a gift called life and I will never take for granted, but always cherish this gift, because I know that Jesus freely gave His life for mine."

"For God so loved the world, that he gave his only begotten Son, that whosoever believeth in him should not perish, but have everlasting life."
— John 3:16 (KJV)

What Others are Saying

"Jacob has held a special place in my heart since first meeting him. He gains his strength from Christ and follows the plans He has for him diligently. Jacob is full of faith and spiritually gifted to spread The Truth. He is an inspiration. Being a friend to Jacob Berry is a privilege and just knowing him is a blessing." — *Stacey Cummins, Briar's Mom*

"Jacob Berry is a true hero to me and so many others he has touched. My visits with Jacob over the years have inspired me to be a better person. His positive attitude and love of people is contagious and he sends a message to all of us that regardless of what hurdles we face in life we can overcome and help others. —*Steve Owens, Friend and '69 Heisman Winner*

"I met Jacob Berry six years ago at a camp meeting in Seffner Florida. Years later he preached a message and at his altar call I found myself on my knees asking God's forgiveness for not being as thankful as I should for my many blessings. He inspired me so much that I wrote a song about this young courageous man and how his humble words and perseverance changed my way of thinking and caused me to realize 'I'm Blessed.' I highly recommend this young man and his book. He is truly sharing and living the gift. I love you Jacob." — *Tammy Jones Robinette*

To order more *Living the Gift* books
or to discover other resources by
Jacob Berry, please visit:

www.JacobBerryMinistries.org